INTRODUCTION

Life today moves fast. Somewhere between deadlines, expectation, bills, relationship and endless notifications, we've lost touch with peace. We don't pause and we don't feel truly seen in our struggles.

That's why *Stress Research India* created this book- **100 STORIES TO HELP REDUCE YOUR STRESS** – not as a lecture, but as a lifeline. These stories are small, but their impact is deep. They come from real moments, real people, real emotions – stories that make you feel less alone and more human.

Each one is just 200 words – a gentle nudge, a new way of seeing, a tiny shift in mindset that could make a big difference. Whether you are struggling at work, drowning in family pressure, battling anxiety, or just feeling lost – you will find part of yourself in these pages.

These stories don't solve your life. But soften it. They guide you back to your center. Read them slowly. Let them sink in. Let it be your daily dose of peace. You deserve to live a little lighter. Sometimes, the smallest stories heal the biggest wounds.

100 Stories To Help You Reduce Stress
Guruprasad Shetty

Published in 2025

© Published by

Qurate
quratebooks.com

Qurate Books Pvt. Ltd.
Goa 403523, India
www.quratebooks.com
Tel: 1800-210-6527, Email: info@quratebooks.com

ISBN: 978-93-58980-68-4

Contents

UNDERSTANDING STRESS

MINDSET SHIFTS

PRACTICAL TECHNIQUES

RELATIONSHIP STRESS

FAMILY AND PARENTING STRESS

MENTAL AND EMOTIONAL MANAGEMENT

PURPOSE AND MEANING

RESILIENCE STORIES

100 STORIES TO HELP YOU REDUCE YOUR STRESS

Is your daily dose of calm, clarity and courage-told through powerful relatable stories that heal and uplift. Divided into **ten life-changing sections,** this book covers major source of modern stress: 1) Understanding stress 2) Mindset Shifts 3) Practical Techniques 4) Work-Related Stress 5) Financial Stress 6) Relationship Stress 7) Family and Parenting Stress 8) Mental and Emotional Management 9) Purpose and Meaning 10) Resilience Stories

Each section contains 10 bite-sized stories, just 200 words each, offering big value in a small format. These are aren't just stories but solution to stress explained in story format. Whether you are battling burnout, relationship tension, parenting fatigue or financial anxiety, this book offers insight, comfort, clarity.

These are adult bedtime stories, crafted to calm your mind, ease you into peace and gently wean you off the blue light from digital devices that can disrupt your sleep.

JOIN THE MOVEMENT TO HEAL A STRESSED WORLD

Stress Research India (SRI) is on heartfelt mission to reduce stress by awakening the higher human within us all. Stress is often triggered by our lower brain – our survival instinct – when life feels threatened, uncertain or out of control. But there is hope. By shifting our mindset, we can transform stress into strength. At SRI we teach how to *reframe challenges as tests of human spirit,* and to respond like SRI humans – **Sensible, Rational, Intelligent** not react like threatened animals fight-or-flight.

Through talks, seminars, and workshops, we equip individuals to replace panic with purpose, helplessness with action, and confusion with clarity. You can also train to become a **Stress Support Guide** – someone who listens, counsels, leads others to calm using our proven SRI methods. This is more than a program – it's a path to personal healing and social change.

Be the calm this chaotic world needs. Email: stressresearchindia@gmail.com

"Your Review means a lot ! Kindly share it on Amazon to help others discover this book" - Guru

1.

WHY AM I SO STRESSED?

Ria stared at her overflowing inbox. Her boss had snapped at her. A teammate missed a deadline. Her breath quickened." Why am I so stressed?" She muttered.

That evening, she met Guru. He smiled gently, "Ria, your stress isn't weakness. It is your lower brain trying to protect you."

He continued, "We all have an animal brain - the lower part - which gets triggered when it senses something we don't like, feel uncertain about, or can't control. It perceives such situations as threats and automatically prepares the body to fight or flee. That's why your heart races, breath shortens, and muscles tighten. In ancient times, this helped animals survive predators. But today, we face psychological threats – pressure, setbacks, criticism - not physical danger. Still, the brain triggers stress."

"So, what can I do?" Ria asked. "Use your higher brain – your intellect," Guru replied. "Recognize that problems are no threats, but challenges. You can't change your biology, but you can change your psychology. Accept, reflect, respond. Don't take things personally or feel bad. Stay solution-focused."

Ria took a deep breath. It made sense. She couldn't stop stress being triggered-but she could stop it from taking over.

2.

HOW CAN I REDUCE STRESS?

Ria slumped into the chair across from Guru, eyes tired, voice tense. "How can I reduce stress, Guru? I feel like I'm always reacting - snapping at colleagues, overthinking, losing sleep. Guru sipped his tea, then said gently, "You are getting stressed because you're forgetting to be human."

Ria frowned. "I am human."

Guru smiled. "Yes, but when there are problems and challenges, your lower brain, the animal brain takes over. It reacts like an animal: emotional, defensive, impulsive. It triggers stress and creates an urge in your body to fight or run as it perceives problems and challenges as threats to your life. If there is something that you don't like, your lower brain may perceive the same as danger and react"

"So, what do I do? she asked.

"You remember the human in you - the upper brain, that can pause, reason, reflect and respond. You don't fight problems and challenges. You respond to them, sensibly, rationally and intelligently." Guru said. Start with awareness, when stress arises, observe it. Don't let the animal in you react. Identify what the underlying thoughts are and note what is bothering you and work out response.

The next day, when a meeting turned tense. Ria noticed her racing thoughts; she didn't speak immediately. She paused, relaxed and replied calmly. It felt powerful because she was in control now.

3.

HOW CAN I SOLVE MY PROBLEM?

Guru, how can I solve my problem? Ria asked. Guru smiled and said "You cannot solve a problem by becoming an animal - reacting with stress, fight, or flight. To solve a problem, you must be human - sensible, rational, and intelligent."

The first step to solving any problem is *acceptance.* Resistance only creates stress and blocks clarity. Acceptance clears the mind and frees your intellect to reason, reflect and respond.

Some problems have immediate solutions. Some need time, effort, and patience. And some may have no perfect solutions - yet they can still be managed. Unlike animals with limited options, humans have *multiple choices:* accept, act, adjust, adapt, alter, avoid, or adjourn.

Use logical thinking, explore problem solving techniques and remember - you're not the first person to face this challenge. Millions have gone through similar issues. Books, videos, and online resources can guide and inspire.

Talk to family or friends - they may see things more clearly since they're emotionally detached. Seek help of a therapist consultant or counselor if needed. Trust the process. Most problems don't last forever. With calmness and consistent effort, solutions always emerge. Just keep moving forward with clarity and courage.

4.

MY BOSS IS STRESSING ME

Ravi was a senior analyst in a reputed firm. His new boss, Mr. Sharma, was a nightmare – constantly shifting deadlines, unclear instructions, public criticism, and unrealistic targets. Ravi felt trapped, he couldn't afford to quit as an education loan and home loan weighed on him.

One evening, after another harsh meeting, Ravi met Guru at stress workshop. Guru listened quietly and said," You can't control Mr. Sharma, but you can control how you respond. Right now, you're reacting from your lower brain – fight or flight. But you can rise higher." Guru continued, "When you feel provoked, pause. Take reverse breath, that is first exhale and then inhale. Refuse to let someone else's behaviour decide your mood. Be SRI – Sensible, Rational, Intelligent."

Ravi began practicing emotional detachment. He documented all tasks, calmly sought clarifications through emails. He stopped taking Mr. Sharma's tone personally. He started saving bit by bit to build buffer. In few months, Ravi noticed something shift – his health improved, anxiety dropped, and Mr. Sharma began respecting his calm composure. Ravi hadn't changed his boss. He had changed his response.

Guru's words echoed in his mind: "Don't let someone else's pressure become your stress. Stay Strong. Be "SRI."

5.

RECOGNIZING THE SYMPTOMS

Aditi asked Guru, "How can I reduce stress?"

"Being aware of the symptoms of stress is the first step towards reducing it. When the body is under stress, it exhibits distinct symptoms," Guru replied.

- **Physical symptoms:** Shallow breathing, increased heart rate, muscle tension, headaches, high blood pressure.
- **Emotional symptoms:** Fear, anxiety, anger, aggression, restlessness, persistent worry, and feeling overwhelmed.
- **Mental symptoms:** Racing thoughts, difficulty concentrating, constant distractions, forgetfulness, mental fog, rumination.
- **Behavioral symptoms:** Avoidance, isolation, procrastination, disorganization, impulsivity, erratic behavior, substance abuse (alcohol, drugs, smoking).

If you recognize any of these symptoms, it's a sign that your body is in stress mode—gearing up to fight or flee. But remember, this instinctive response doesn't serve us in today's world; instead, it can harm us.

A very simple way to regain control over you is to use the *cool down technique*. In this technique, you breathe out deeply through your mouth, which forces you to take a deeper breath through your nose. When you exhale fully, the carbon dioxide in your lungs is released completely. Once your lungs are empty, you naturally inhale more deeply, bringing in more oxygen. This increased oxygen calms your nerves and helps you relax.

6.

THE ISSUE ABOUT STRESS

"The issue with stress is that it gets triggered automatically," Guru explained to his trainees. "The moment our senses detect something threatening, the brain signals the body — faster heartbeat, tightened muscles, shallow breathing — all without asking us. This helped early humans survive danger, but today, most of our problems aren't life-threatening."

He paused. "Yet the brain still reacts as if they are. A difficult boss, a late payment, or an argument at home can trigger the same stress response that once helped us escape a tiger."

Guru continued, "This overreaction isn't helpful. It raises blood pressure, weakens immunity, causes ulcers, and slowly damages the body. We can't stop our automatic nervous system or avoid life's problems."

He smiled gently. "But we can become more aware. We can notice the signs of stress early, pause, and respond wisely. With practice, we can use simple techniques — like breathing, reflection, or movement — to calm the body. Most importantly, we can use our intelligence, not just instinct, to face challenges. Stress may be automatic, but our response can be deliberate."

7.

HOW JOE BUILT UP STRESS IN HIS BODY

Joe woke up late and immediately became upset — he had an important meeting. He rushed to take a bath but found the water cold, which made him even more frustrated. Irritated, he yelled at his wife because breakfast wasn't ready. She got upset too, which made Joe even more agitated.

He rushed out but got stuck in a traffic jam, fuming with impatience. When he finally reached the office, his bosses yelled at him, making Joe feel insecure about his job. To release his frustration, he yelled at his subordinates, upsetting them — and himself — all over again.

By now, Joe could feel his blood pressure rising. His heart was racing, his head was throbbing, and his entire body felt tense. His mind was clouded with anger and worry, making it difficult to focus on work. At night, he couldn't sleep because of recurring thoughts, and the next morning, he woke up with a headache from lack of rest.

Joe unknowingly turned small inconveniences into major stressors, harming both his body and mind. A better response would have been to accept the situation, adapt, and move forward. Instead of wasting energy on frustration, he could have adjusted, corrected, and continued — without making things worse for himself and those around him.

8.

STRESS DEFUSING TECHNIQUES

Joe asked Guru for quick stress-control techniques that would work in real-life situations at work. Guru shared a few effective methods:

1. **Change Thought Technique:** Replace stressful thoughts with calming ones. Shift your focus to something positive or neutral to break the stress cycle.
2. **Self-Talk Technique:** Talk to yourself calmly — "Stay in control," "Don't react," "This will pass." Self-instructions help regulate emotional responses.
3. **Cool Down Technique:** Exhale deeply and then inhale slowly. Taking a few deep breaths helps lower stress and brings instant relaxation.
4. **Awareness & Labelling:** Recognize when stress is building up. Label the emotions—anger, frustration, anxiety. Naming them reduces their grip.
5. **Walking Away:** Step away from arguments, toxic people, workplace conflicts, or distressing news. Creating distance helps you regain composure.
6. **Physical Release:** Splash cold water on your face, massage your temples or the top of your head. Simple physical actions can ease tension.

Joe found these techniques easy and practical. He started using them and experienced better control over workplace stress.

9.

STOP SHOUTING

This happened in Mumbai. Shefali Ranjan, 42, a loving but anxious mother had one dream — to see her 21-year-old son, Vedant, become a successful IT engineer like her cousin in the U.S. But Vedant's heart beat for music.

Shefali pushed hard — tuitions, report cards, teachers' meetings. But Vedant felt like a failure in a life that wasn't his. While his mother prayed for marks, he spent days in Andheri studios, writing rap songs no one at home understood.

One evening, Vedant returned without his mark sheet. Shefali scolded him, followed him to his room, banging on the door he had locked behind him.

Inside, Vedant was spiraling. Her voice became a storm in his head, her words — knives.

And then, in a terrifying snap of rage, he grabbed a real knife from the kitchen.

Shefali didn't even scream. Forty-two wounds. Blood everywhere.

When it was done, he dipped his finger in her blood and wrote on the wall:

"STOP SHOUTING. CATCH ME. HANG ME."

In one tragic minute — a mother died, a son broke, a father was destroyed, and a family became a headline.

Unaddressed stress doesn't just hurt. Sometimes, it kills.

10.

THE ANIMAL AND HUMAN WITHIN – DUALITY IN THE BRAIN

Guru stood before a group of senior leaders and said, "Understanding this duality in our brain will help you master stress and emotional intelligence."

He continued, "Think of your brain as having two parts. The lower part — called the 'animal brain' — includes the reptilian brain and the limbic system. It's ancient, emotional, and reactive. This part of the brain controls fear, anger, and survival instincts. It's fast and automatic, like an animal reacting to danger. That's why, when we feel threatened, this part takes over and triggers stress — preparing us to fight, freeze, or run.

Above this sits the 'human brain' — the rational, thinking part. It helps us pause, reflect, reason, and respond. It developed later in evolution and is what makes us truly human.

But here's the twist: all information goes through the animal brain first. If it senses a threat, it hijacks the system before the human brain can even think. That's why stress can feel instant and uncontrollable.

Emotional intelligence is the art of recognizing when we're in 'animal mode' and choosing to shift to 'human mode.' Being reactive is easy. Being wise requires awareness and conscious effort. That's the journey from stress to strength."

11.

THE RADIO INSIDE

Arjun sat quietly, head down, lost in thought.

"Guru," he whispered, "my mind keeps criticizing me — *'You're not good enough.'* It never stops."

Guru smiled gently and pointed to a small radio nearby. "This radio plays whatever frequency it's tuned to. If it's on a negative station, what do we hear?"

"Negative voices. Complaints. Doubt," Arjun replied.

"Exactly," Guru said. "Now, imagine your mind is like that radio. The negative voice? That's an old station running on autopilot. But here's the magic — you can speak louder from outside and tune into a new frequency."

"But how?"

"Deliberate positive self-talk," Guru said. "Speak kindly to yourself — out loud or silently. Say things like *'I'm good. I'm learning. I'm growing.'* At first, it feels fake. But if you keep repeating it, it becomes your new station."

Arjun frowned. "But won't the old station come back?"

"Yes," Guru nodded. "But now you know you have the remote. You shift your mindset from victimhood to confidence. Over time, your chosen voice becomes louder, and the old one fades."

Arjun looked up. "So, I don't fight the noise — I replace it."

"Exactly," Guru smiled. "Change the frequency. Change your life."

12.

A SIMPLE SHIFTS

Aditi sat across from Guru, her mind already heavy with worry.

"Let's do a small experiment," Guru said. "For two minutes, think about everything that upsets you — your worries, fears, insecurities. Then observe how you feel."

Aditi closed her eyes and let her mind spiral into her troubles. When she opened them, her face was tense.

"I feel anxious, angry, and stressed," she admitted.

Guru smiled. "Interesting. Nothing happened in these two minutes, yet you felt worse just by thinking negatively. Now, close your eyes again. This time, think of everything that makes you happy — peaceful moments, joyful memories, dreams that excite you."

Aditi followed his instructions. When she opened her eyes, a smile had replaced her frown.

"I feel calm, happy, and light," she said, surprised.

Guru nodded. "See, nothing around you changed — only your thoughts did. Negative thoughts bring negative feelings, and positive thoughts bring positive feelings. Stress is often not about the situation, but about how we think about it."

A simple technique to control your stress is to **deliberately** think about thoughts that make you feel happy, calm, relaxed, or good. Your brain responds to your **thoughts**, not to the situation. Change your thoughts, and you will change your feelings.

13.

BEING CALM IS NOT SOLVING MY PROBLEM

Aditi sighed, “Guru, I am being calm, but my problem is still there.”

Guru chuckled. “Aditi, being calm won’t magically solve your problems, but it puts you in a better state of mind to handle them.”

He picked up a glass of water. “Imagine this is your mind. When you’re stressed, it’s like adding mud to the water — your thoughts become clouded. Stress tightens your body, raises your blood pressure, and fills your mind with fear, doubt, and anxiety. It becomes hard to focus and think clearly. Even sleep abandons you.”

Aditi nodded. “Yes, that’s exactly how I feel.”

Guru smiled. “Now, what if you get calm? It would settle the mud, making the water clear again. In that clarity, your mind works better — you can reason, reflect, and find solutions.”

Aditi took a deep breath. “So, stress makes problems feel bigger, but a calm mind helps me actually solve them.”

“Exactly,” Guru said. “Choose clarity over chaos.”

14.

NO DISLIKE, NO RESISTANCE + ACCEPTANCE = NO STRESS

Ria asked a deep philosophical question:

"Can there be no stress if there is no dislike, no resistance — only complete acceptance of what is?"

"Yes, it is possible," said the Guru. "Here's why —

Stress arises from the gap between what is and what we want it to be. When we dislike a situation, resist it, or wish it were different, we create internal conflict. This conflict triggers our stress response.

Dislike and resistance fuel the stress response. When we dislike something, we tend to dwell on it, worry about it, and try to avoid it. This constant mental and emotional activity keeps our nervous system in a heightened state. Resistance is essentially fighting against reality — which is inherently draining and stressful.

Acceptance dissolves this conflict. Acceptance doesn't mean liking or condoning everything that happens — it means acknowledging reality as it is. When we accept, the internal battle stops. We are no longer fighting what is. The energy we once spent resisting can now be used to develop more creative, sensible, and intelligent solutions to whatever challenges we face."

15.

HAND IT TO THE UNIVERSE

Laxmi sat on the balcony, staring at the bills in her hands. Her husband's job was uncertain, her son's school fees were due, and the rising expenses felt like an unbearable weight. She had done everything — cut costs, prayed, worried endlessly — but nothing changed. The stress was eating her alive.

That evening, she met Guru at the temple. Seeing her distressed, he asked, "Laxmi, what troubles you?" Tears welled up as she poured out her worries. "I don't know what to do. I feel helpless."

Guru smiled gently. "Not everything is in your hands, Laxmi. Sometimes, you must hand it over to the Universe."

"But how?" she asked.

"Surrender. Trust. Be patient. Have faith. Accept," Guru said. "You've done your best. Now, release the stress of trying to control every outcome."

Laxmi took a deep breath. That night, instead of tossing in anxiety, she whispered, *I hand this to the Universe*.

A few days later, her husband received an unexpected freelance project. It wasn't a miracle, but it was enough. And more importantly, she had found peace — not in solving everything, but in trusting life's flow.

Sometimes, the Universe works when we finally let go.

16.

STRESS IS NOT THE ENEMY

Stress is not the enemy — it's energy. When faced with a challenge, our body releases adrenaline, sharpening focus and boosting drive. If you perceive a situation as a threat, it can trigger fear and anxiety, and the body prepares to fight or flee. But if you perceive the same situation as a challenge, the energy within fuels growth and success.

The situations you face may not be of your own making; they may not be your fault, and you may have no control over them. But modern challenges are not life-threatening—they won't kill you like predators in the wild. They are problems, setbacks, and uncertainties. If you see them as threats, stress will weigh you down. But if you see them as challenges, stress becomes your power.

Sachin Tendulkar didn't choose to get hit by a bouncer that broke his nose, but he chose to stand his ground and build his innings. Dhirubhai Ambani didn't expect to be displaced from Aden, but he turned adversity into opportunity, creating Reliance. Ray Kroc lost his job at the age of 54, but instead of giving up; he took up the challenge and built McDonald's into the world's largest restaurant chain.

Stress is like fire — you can use it, or it can burn you down. Perceiving a demanding situation as a challenge ignites a force within that drives you forward.

17.

ACCEPTANCE

Raj had lost his job. As soon as he heard the news, his heart pounded, his mind raced, and panic set in. He felt crushed, angry, and overwhelmed by fear of the future. That evening, Raj met Guru, who listened calmly and said,

"Raj, your stress is natural — it's your brain's fight-or-flight response trying to protect you. But losing a job is not a threat to your life. What you need now is a shift in how you see this situation. You need to accept the situation and work out solutions instead of resisting, getting upset, angry, or stressed."

Guru continued, "Acceptance does not mean surrender. It means you stop resisting the reality that you can't control. By resisting, you only drain your health and peace. But by accepting the situation, you calm your mind and free up your energy to think clearly."

Raj sat quietly, letting these words sink in. Slowly, his breath softened. Instead of cursing his company or worrying endlessly, he began listing his skills, updating his résumé, and reaching out to his network.

Within weeks, Raj found a new opportunity — even better than his last job.

By shifting from resistance to acceptance, Raj unlocked his ability to respond by being **SRI — Sensible, Rational, and Intelligent** — transforming his stress into purposeful action.

18.

THE BROKEN UMBRELLA

Kris stood at the bus stop, drenched in the unexpected rain. His umbrella had flipped inside out, useless against the heavy downpour. Frustrated, he muttered, "Why does this always happen to me?" His mind raced — he might catch a cold, fall sick, upset his boss, or even be shortlisted for layoff.

Guru, who was standing next to him, was also fully drenched but seemed to be enjoying the rain. Seeing Kris's frustration, he smiled and said, "Shouganai."

Kris frowned. "What?"

Guru smiled and said, *"Shouganai and Ukeireru* are Japanese philosophies that help reduce stress. *Shouganai* means 'it is what it is,' and *Ukeireru* means accepting reality with understanding rather than resistance.

"Some things in life cannot be helped; fighting them only adds to your suffering. Instead of resisting, accept and move forward."

Kris understood. He couldn't change the weather—it was beyond his control. Rather than getting angry, upset, and stressed about it, he could just accept it and move on.

When Kris reached the office, his boss scolded him. Instead of reacting or feeling upset that his boss hadn't appreciated the fact that he came to work despite getting drenched, Kris listened, acknowledged his mistake, didn't make excuses, and moved on — without resentment, without stress.

19.

THE VALUE SHIFT

Rhea, a graphic designer, often felt insecure scrolling through social media.

"Everyone's doing better than me," she thought. She kept constantly chasing what she didn't have — followers, clients, praise — and the insecurity only grew.

One day, Guru told her something simple:
"There are 8 billion people on this planet. With over 8 billion human needs, someone out there needs what you can offer. You're not here to compete; you're here to contribute."

That changed her perspective.
Instead of asking, *"Why don't I have enough?"* she began asking, *"Who needs what I can give?"*

She created a simple service for small businesses — affordable, clean branding. The internet became her marketplace. Fiverr and Freelancer were some of the sites where she listed her work. A school in Kenya, a bakery in Canada, a coach in Delhi — all found her work useful.

She realized there's space for everyone who focuses on serving.

Insecurity faded — not because she became the best, but because she finally stopped comparing and started contributing.
We don't need to be everything to everyone. We just need to be something to someone.

20.

LAW OF ATTRACTION

Malini often felt invisible at work – nervous, under confident, and overlooked for promotions. She believed she wasn't good enough. One day, she heard Guru speak about Law of Attraction and something called the *Reticular Activating System (RAS)* the brain filters and notices what we repeatedly think about.

Your brain focuses on what your mind dwells on, Guru said. "If you keep thinking you are a failure, your brain will seek proof to it everywhere. But if you think and act success, your brain will seek success for you everywhere."

That hit home. Malini decided to shift her inner dialogue. She began practicing positive self-talk, imagining herself speaking confidently, leading meetings, earning praise and being trusted with responsibilities. Slowly she started noticing opportunities she had ignored before – a leadership workshop, a mentor's advice, even subtle encouragement from her boss. Her confidence grew.

A month later, she was invited to present at a high stakes meeting. She prepared thoroughly, spoke with clarity, and impressed everyone. Senior management soon gave her an independent project to lead. Promotion followed. Malini realised success wasn't missing- it was her focus that had been. When she changed her thoughts, her brain began helping her see, seize, and shape her future.

21.

STRESS DAIRY STRATEGY – A PATH TO PEACE

Is there a simple strategy to reduce stress?" Laxmi asked Guru. "Yes," Guru replied. It's called the *Stress Dairy Strategy*. Just one small habit can bring big change."

He explained, "For the next 30 days, every time you feel stressed, pause. Note the situation and your immediate thoughts. Then ask: What would be more *sensible, rational, and intelligent* way to respond instead of reacting automatically?"

"This daily reflection builds awareness. You'll begin noticing patterns – triggers, unhelpful thoughts, and missed opportunities for calm responses." Guru, then shared the powerful **7 A's** – a guide to navigate stressful moments:

1. **Accept** what you cannot change.
2. **Act** on what you can change.
3. **Adjust** when needed.
4. **Adapt** when required.
5. **Alter** to your advantage.
6. **Avoid** stressing over small stuff.
7. **Adjourn** your response – time heals.

Laxmi smiled. "That sounds doable." Guru nodded, it's not magic, it's mindset. You train your brain to respond, not react. And in that space between stimulus and response – you find peace.

22.

THE SRI APPROACH

Aditi was overwhelmed. Her company was downsizing, and anxiety consumed her. Sleepless nights, worry, and fear took over. She turned to her guide, Guru.

He listened calmly and said, "In every difficult situation, remember the *SRI Approach* – Be **Sensible, Rational,** and **Intelligent**. It works in every area of life.

"Let's apply it to your situation," he continued. "Your company is downsizing. The problem: your job may be at risk. Now ask – what is the *Sensible* thing to do? Accept the reality without panic." The *Rational* thing? Asses your finances, identify your skills, update your resume, reach out to contacts. The *Intelligent thing?* Start preparing for interviews, explore alternate opportunities, and invest in upgrading your knowledge. Think ahead, don't freeze in fear."

Guru smiled gently. "Stress weakens you. SRI strengthens you. Choose to respond – not react."

Aditi took a deep breath. The situation hadn't changed, but something inside her had. She now had a method, a mindset, and a mirror to reflect her strength.

23.

THREE MANTRAS TO REDUCE STRESS

Ronnie, trapped in a toxic work environment, felt his confidence crumbling. His new supervisor's manipulative tactics and constant gas lighting pushed him to the brink. Ready to resign, he sought help from Guru and his team. Guru offered three powerful mantras for stress reduction.

MANTRA 1: "I WILL NOT BE AN ANIMAL."

This addressed the instinctive fight-or-flight response triggered by stress. By recognizing the physical signs of stress and repeating this mantra, Ronnie could consciously choose not to react impulsively.

MANTRA 2: "I WILL NOT HURT MYSELF."

This mantra focused on the physical toll of stress. By affirming that he wouldn't harm his health, Ronnie indirectly committed to managing his stress levels, mitigating the damaging effects of elevated blood pressure and other stress-related issues.

MANTRA 3: "I WILL BE SRI."

This mantra empowered Ronnie to maintain emotional control. By reminding himself to be Sensible, Rational, and Intelligent (SRI), he could resist manipulation and provocation, finding solutions through calm and composed thinking.

These mantras helped Ronnie regain his composure and navigate the stressful situation with clarity.

24.

STRESS RELIEF THROUGH JOURNALING

Shilpi, a marketing professional, often felt overwhelmed by deadlines, client demands, and constant pressure at work. Her mind was cluttered with worries, and stress kept her awake at night. One day, she came across the idea of journaling and decided to give it a try.

Each night, she sat in a quiet corner with her journal and wrote down everything that was bothering her. As she put her thoughts on paper, she realized that many of her fears were exaggerated. Writing helped her process emotions, organize her thoughts, and identify solutions.

For example, when she felt anxious about an upcoming presentation, she listed her concerns and brainstormed ways to prepare better. This gave her a sense of control and reduced her stress. Over time, she noticed a change — her thoughts became clearer, she slept better, and she felt more in charge of her emotions.

Journaling became her daily habit — a safe space where she could unload her thoughts without judgment. While it didn't reduce her workload, it transformed how she handled stress. With a calmer mind, she became more productive and resilient, proving that a simple practice could make a profound difference.

25.

YOG NIDRA

Sid approached Guru, a Stress Support Guide. “Guru, I can’t sleep well, and my mind is always racing. Can you teach me Yog Nidra?” he asked.

Guru smiled and gestured for Sid to lie down comfortably. In a soft, meditative voice, he guided, “Close your eyes and bring your awareness to your breath. Feel the air as it flows in and out. Now, with each breath, silently utter the mantra: *Relax... Relax... Relax...”*

As Sid followed the instructions, Guru directed his awareness to different parts of the body:
“Bring your attention to the top of your head. Whisper to it: *Relax... Relax... Relax...”*
Slowly, he guided Sid through his forehead, eyes, jaw, shoulders, hands, legs, back, and entire body, repeating the mantra at each step. With every breath, tension melted away, and Sid felt himself drifting into deep relaxation.

As Sid awoke, refreshed, Guru explained, “Yog Nidra is a powerful relaxation practice. It reduces stress, calms anxiety, lowers blood pressure, and improves sleep. By activating the parasympathetic nervous system, it counteracts the stress response, bringing deep rest and healing to both body and mind. You can practice it yourself every night.”

Sid smiled, feeling lighter than he had in years.

26.

GROUNDING TECHNIQUE – A SIMPLE WAY TO REGAIN FOCUS

Sid rushed to Guru and said, “I’m totally distracted at work. My mind’s all over the place. I need a quick fix!”

Guru smiled and said, “Try the grounding technique.”

“What’s that?” Sid asked.

“It’s a way to bring your mind back to the present moment. Here’s a simple version,” Guru explained.

“Sit comfortably. Take a deep breath. Now, look around and name:

- 5 things you can see.
- 4 things you can touch.
- 3 things you can hear.
- 2 things you can smell.
- 1 thing you can taste.

This is called the **5-4-3-2-1 method**. It uses your senses to pull you back to the ‘now’. When your brain is running wild, grounding slows it down. You become calmer and more focused.”

Whenever your mind is racing or you feel lost in stress, use this technique. It works anywhere – at your desk, in a meeting, while travelling, etc.

27.

5-MINUTE MIND RESET

Aditi, an advertising manager, was drowning in deadlines. She felt her stress rising before an important presentation. Instead of panicking, she tried a simple meditation technique – the **5-Minute Mind Reset**.

She sat in a quiet corner, closed her eyes, and focused on her breath.
Inhale... 1...2...3...4...

Exhale... 4...3...2...1...

With each breath, she imagined stress leaving her body like dark smoke. Her heartbeat slowed. Thoughts of failure and pressure faded.

Then, she placed her hand on her heart and whispered,
"I am capable. I am calm. I am enough."
Repeating this affirmation synced her mind and body, replacing stress with clarity.

Five minutes later, she opened her eyes. The chaos in her mind had settled. She walked into the meeting room feeling centered and confident.

This meditation works because it combines **deep breathing, visualization,** and **affirmations**. Whenever stress strikes, pause, breathe, and reset your mind.

Try it now – close your eyes, breathe deeply, and feel the tension melt away.

28.

MINDFULNESS TO REDUCE STRESS

Raj asked Guru, "Nowadays, we hear so much about mindfulness. What is it, and how does it reduce stress?"

Guru smiled. "Mindfulness is the ability to be fully present in the moment — aware of your body, thoughts, and sensations — a witness, detached and non-judgmental. When you observe without reacting, stress loses its grip on you."

Mindful Thinking:
Close your eyes and simply observe your thoughts. Don't react, analyze, or judge — just be aware. As you watch them pass like clouds, their intensity fades, and your mind becomes still.

Mindful Breathing:
Inhale slowly, visualizing cool blue air entering your body, clearing all blocks as it fills your lungs. Exhale gently, imagining stress and toxins leaving with your breath. Continue for 10–15 minutes, feeling lighter with each breath.

"You can practice mindfulness in everything — eating, walking, even drinking tea," Guru added. "Be fully present. Taste, feel, and experience each moment. When you are mindful, you are in control, no longer lost in worries. In that space of awareness, stress dissolves effortlessly."

Raj nodded, as a sense of calm washed over him. He had found a simple yet powerful way to reclaim peace.

29.

REPLACING NEGATIVE THOUGHTS

Anaya, a young marketing executive, constantly felt like a fraud at work. Every small mistake seemed to confirm her fear: *"I am not good enough"* Her inner critic grew louder by the day.

She met Guru, who listened patiently. "Anaya," he said gently, "what we say to ourselves is often more damaging than what others say about us. The animal in us has habit of self-criticism."

He asked her to list her negative thoughts and question each one: *"What evidence do you have for this?"* Most were just feelings – not facts. Guru gave her an assignment: For the next month, catch every negative thought and replace it with a rational one. Change 'I will fail' to 'I have prepared well. 'Replace I'm not good enough' with I'm learning and getting better every day.

Anaya took it seriously. Slowly the spiral of self-doubt turned into a ladder of self-belief. Her confidence grew, and her work reflected it. She told Guru, "I couldn't silence the voice- but I stopped believing it."

Guru smiled," Exactly. Don't believe everything your mind tells you. Train it. Remember, your mind should be your servant – not your master.

30.

TOOLKIT TO MANAGE STRESS

Kevin felt overwhelmed. His mind was a battlefield of negative thoughts, emotions and reactions.

Seeing his struggle, Guru said, "Kevin, stress is a natural response, but it doesn't have to control you. Your autonomic nervous system sees threats everywhere, but unchecked stress often creates more harm than good. You need a **toolkit** to manage it."

Here's what Guru suggested:

- **Remind yourself to be human** – Don't react like an animal.
- **Change your thoughts to change your feelings.**
- **Journal and release unhelpful thoughts.**
- **Reframe your thoughts** – See the situation as a challenge, not a threat.
- **Cool down before reacting** – Breathe, pause, and avoid impulsive reactions.
- **Find solutions** – Take action instead of endlessly worrying.
- **Accept, avoid, adjust, or adapt** – Don't resist reality.
- **Be your own friend** – Be mindful of your self-talk.
- **Exercise, meditate, and sleep well** – Strengthen both body and mind.
- **Share your stress** – Talking lightens the load.

Kevin smiled. Now he had a plan—not just to survive stress, but to master it.

31.

STRESS REDUCTION AT WORK

Amit, a hardworking professional, often felt overwhelmed at work. His to-do list was endless, and deadlines loomed like dark clouds.

One day, his mentor Eric shared some simple but powerful advice:

"Prioritize wisely," Eric said. "Not everything is urgent. What's important to you might not be a priority for your boss. Focus on the 20% of tasks that bring 80% of the results. Delegate the rest."

Amit realized he had been trying to do everything himself.

Eric continued, **"Time is your asset. Set fixed slots for emails and messages to avoid constant distractions. Learn to say NO. Protect your work hours from unnecessary interruptions."** Amit started setting boundaries and noticed he was more productive.

"Criticism will come," Eric said, **"but don't let it provoke you. Stay calm, focus on what's useful, and ignore the rest."** Amit practiced this approach and felt less stressed.

Eric also suggested taking five-minute breaks, stretching regularly, and communicating when overwhelmed. Amit found that sharing with a trusted colleague lightened his burden. By eating on time, sleeping well, and taking breaks, he finally felt in control.

Work pressure didn't vanish — but stress no longer controlled him.

32.

BURN OUT TO BALANCE

Simran, a passionate interior designer, once loved her work. But endless meetings, tight deadlines, demanding clients, payment delays and sleepless nights had drained her. She felt burned out. She met Guru. Together, they created a plan using SRI approach – Be **Sensible, Rational** and **Intelligent**.

Meetings: Only essential meetings would be in person. Each meeting would have a clear agenda and a fixed time. Time exceeds; Simran would excuse herself politely.

Deadlines: She learned to say "No" to unrealistic deadlines. Instead, she promised what was reasonable – and delivered early to delight her clients.

Documentation: Every meeting now had minutes. If clients changed requirements, she documented the scope, cost, and time impact – to avoid future disputes.

Payment Terms: She stopped taking Turnkey projects. Instead, she had two agreements – one for her design and consultancy fees, and separate tripartite agreement (Client, Contractor, Herself) for execution. This ensured transparency and timely payments.

The result? Simran work- life balance improved. No more unnecessary stress, financial risk, or last-minute chaos. She reclaimed her peace, focus and creativity. Guru smiled, "Stress fades when you take charge with sense, reason, and intelligence." Simran finally felt alive, doing what she loved, without burning out.

33.

BREAKING FREE FROM THE TOXIC WORK TRAP

Venky was once the star performer at his company. But things changed when his boss quit, and the new boss brought in his own team. The new boss micromanaged every task, and the team thrived on gossip and office politics. The unrealistic demands and deadlines were draining. Each morning, Venky dreaded going to the office.

One evening, exhausted and frustrated, he spoke to Guru. Guru reminded him to respect his strengths and added, "The Company needs you as much as you need the company. Make yourself so valuable that you're worth more than what they pay. If you're truly valuable, others will want to hire you too. Be sensible, rational, and use your intelligence."

Venky got the message. He set clear boundaries and simplified his work. He reflected on what truly mattered—his health and happiness. Calmly and rationally, he explained why the current demands were unrealistic. He expressed his concerns and subtly let it be known that he was open to better opportunities.

Gradually, the weight lifted. He stopped seeking validation from his toxic boss and colleagues. He prioritized his well-being and his work. His boss, fearing further attrition, became more realistic and began respecting employees' well-being. Eventually, management, having noticed the high attrition rate and departmental issues, sacked the toxic boss—and promoted Venky to the role he rightfully deserved.

34.

WORK-LIFE BALANCE

Jia, a high-achieving lawyer, lived on deadlines and caffeine. She worked late nights, skipped meals, and barely saw her family. Stress had become her constant companion, leading to exhaustion, irritability, and feelings of loneliness. Her hectic schedule had even led to a separation from her husband.

One day, after missing the Parent-Teacher Meeting at her son's school, she felt guilty and bought an expensive toy for him. But her six-year-old refused it and said, "Mama, I don't want the toy, I want you."

Her heart sank. In that moment, she realized that her family's happiness mattered far more than the fat paycheck at the law firm.

She decided to become sensible, rational, and intelligent about her work so she could maintain a better work-life balance.

Jia began taking on only high-value work, reducing the quantity so that quality could improve. Client calls were restricted to office hours. Matters were to be submitted in advance so her team could prepare opinions and strategies. Weekends were reserved for family, and one day a week, she worked from home. Stress Buster Meetups by the Stress Support Guide were held regularly in her office.

Her efforts paid off. One day, her six-year-old hugged her tightly and said, "Mama, I'm so happy." Jia was also pleasantly surprised when her estranged spouse called to ask her out for a dinner date.

35.

REDUCE STRESS DURING LONG WORKING HOURS

Rohan, a corporate lawyer, often worked 12-14 hours a day. Exhausted and edgy, he asked Guru, "How can I reduce stress with such long hours?" Guru smiled, "You can't always shorten your workday, but you can reduce stress during it. Here are 10 sensible, rational, and intelligent (SRI) ways."

Start with Silence: Begin your day with 5 minutes of calm breathing or silence before switching on devices. *Prioritize Task:* Identify 3 key tasks for the day. Complete them first. *Micro-Breaks:* Take a 5-minute break every hour- stretch, walk, or close your eyes. *Hydrate & Nourish:* Drink water regularly. Eat light, energy–sustaining meals. *Mini Meditation:* Two minutes of mindfulness at your desk to reset mind. *Clear Clutter:* A clean workspace reduces mental fatigue. *Positive Triggers:* Keep a photo, quote or object that uplifts you near your desk. *Screen-Free Lunch:* Eat mindfully, not in front of screens. *Manage Thoughts:* Negative thoughts, replace them with constructive ones. *End Smart:* Wind down with a to-do list, leave work at work.

Guru smiled, "You can't always control your hours- but you can control how you feel within them. Make yourself feel good; your body would reduce feeling bad.

36.

UNCLEAR EXPECTATIONS

Aman had just started a new job. His boss gave him a project but provided little direction. Every time Aman asked for clarity, the response was vague: "Figure it out." Aman felt anxious, second-guessing every decision. The stress of not knowing what was expected drained his energy.

One evening, he attended a Stress Support Meet up and shared his concerns with Guru. Guru listened patiently and said, "be sensible, rational, and use your intelligence."

Aman was confused, so Guru explained, "Think of this lack of clarity like driving in fog. You don't stop — you slow down, turn on your headlights, and confirm you're headed in the right direction. Do the same here: break the task into small steps, confirm each part, and document everything."

The next day, Aman made a simple change. He summarized his understanding of the project in an email and sent it to his boss: *"This is what I plan to do. Let me know if I should adjust anything."* To his surprise, his boss responded: *"Looks good. Just add this one thing."*

Aman realized that waiting for perfect clarity was pointless. By taking small, clear steps and seeking confirmation, he reduced his stress and made progress. Later, he was pleasantly surprised to learn from HR that his boss had described him as someone who *takes initiative, is self-motivated, and shows leadership potential.*

37.

THE LAYOFF SCARE

Subbu's heart raced as he scrolled through his work chat—another round of layoffs. His fingers trembled as he refreshed his inbox, dreading the email that might end his job. He had loans, and responsibilities. *What if I'm next?*

He called Guru.

"Breathe, Subbu," Guru said. "Even if the worst happens, you'll figure it out."

"I don't know," Subbu replied. "What if I'm not good enough to get another job?"

Guru chuckled. "Seriously? You've solved impossible problems at work. You helped the team when no one else could. Do you really think that suddenly you mean nothing? Value yourself. You're more than your job."

Subbu paused. He had created solutions, led projects, and built systems that added real value. His skills hadn't vanished because of layoffs.

"What if," Guru continued, "you saw this moment as proof that it's time to trust yourself? Companies change, but your ability to create value doesn't."

The next day, when the email finally arrived, Subbu's stomach tightened. But this time, a different thought emerged: *"I am more than a job title. I create value wherever I go."*

Instead of panic, he felt something new — **Confidence.** He wasn't just waiting for security anymore; he was ready to build it.

38.

HANDLING WORKPLACE GASLIGHTING

Nicky had just transitioned from a top law firm to the HR department of reputed multinational. Intelligent, diligent and full of ideas, she quickly gained appreciation – especially when she flawlessly implemented the POSCO rules. But her immediate boss, who lacked legal training and had climbed the ladder by networking, felt threatened.

He began gas lighting her subtly. “Your ideas are good, but not practical,” he would murmur with a smile that masked insecurity. He insisted on reviewing all her work, nitpicked endlessly and slowly eroded her confidence. Nicky began to second-guess herself, stayed up late rechecking her work, and even considered quitting a job she actually loved.

That’s when she met Guru. He listened patiently and then smiled. “Nicky you’re being gas lighted. Don’t let someone else rewrite your worth. When someone tries to shake your confidence, just smile. Don’t react. That confuses manipulators.

Empowered, Nicky stopped defending herself. In the next meeting, when her boss subtly undermined her, she simply smiled. The HR Director, observing silently all along, smiled back.

A week later, the manipulative manager was transferred to a remote unit. Nicky was promoted as HR Head for Management, Marketing, Sales and Admin Staff. Her calm dignity had won.

39.

A LESS STRESS DAY

Sid asked Guru, "How can I have a day without stress?"

Guru smiled, "Sid, stress is not the real problem. It's your biological reaction to the problem. If you adopt the *SRI approach* – be **Sensible, Rational,** and **Intelligent** – you can create a less-stress day." He continued, "Wake up early and begin the day in calm. Have a simple plan- know what you need to do. Accept that there will be delays, demands, and disturbances. That's life. Don't react. ***Pause.***"

When something upsets you, don't let your animal brain take over. Don't allow the body to get stressed, fight or flight. **Reason, Reflect,** and **Respond.** That small space between stimulus and response – that where peace begins.

Remember, you can't control others, but you can control yourself. Choose your response. Stay calm even when people around you are not. Most importantly, take care of *yourself before* trying to take care of work. Eat well, breathe deep, take short breaks, and sleep on time. Your body is your anchor-protect it.

Guru concluded, "A less stress day isn't about a perfect day. It's about the wiser way of living it. If you feel bad, there is stress, if you don't feel bad, there is no stress."

40.

THE DEADLINE TRAP

Kavya was the most sincere member of her team. That's exactly why her boss always dropped urgent work on her desk at 6:00 PM.

One Friday evening, just as she was about to leave for her friend's birthday, the boss casually said, "The client needs this by morning. I trust you'll manage." No discussion, no apology — just pressure, as always.

Kavya's chest tightened. The old thoughts returned: Why me? What if I say no? Will I be seen as difficult? Her body tensed; her heart raced.

But this time, she paused. She remembered the **SRI** mindset.

She became **Sensible:** *This is not the first time. It's a pattern.*
She became **Rational:** *I've done this before, only to find out on Monday that it wasn't urgent — the client would have waited if we had said no.*
She became **intelligent:** She calmly replied, "I can do this first thing Monday. Tonight, I have a commitment I can't miss."

And she chose to be **SRI** — the higher person — not reacting with anger, not shrinking with fear, but standing her ground with dignity. Her boss stared, surprised. But Kavya smiled and left.

That night, the weight in her chest was gone. The stress hadn't disappeared — she had simply stopped feeding it with her inability to say *no.*

41.

THE SECRET TO FINANCIAL PEACE

Ravi sat across from Guru, his face lined with worry. "Guru, there's so much uncertainty in my job. How will I pay my bills if I lose it?"

Guru smiled gently. "Ravi, do you remember the squirrel?"

Ravi frowned. "The squirrel?"

"Yes," Guru nodded. "The squirrel gathers nuts all summer, preparing for winter. It never panics when the cold arrives."

Ravi sighed. "I wish I had prepared."

Guru tapped the table. "It's not too late. Let's start now. First, build an emergency fund — six months of expenses. Next, spend less than you earn. Save before you spend. Income may stop, but expenses don't. Use credit wisely. Pay bills on time to build trust. And always protect yourself — health insurance can save you from financial disaster."

Ravi nodded. "But what if I lose my job?"

Guru smiled. "Job security is a myth. Your real security lies in your skills, your network, and your ability to create value. The more valuable you are, the more opportunities will find you."

Ravi's shoulders relaxed. He had a plan. Financial peace wasn't about earning more — it was about making smarter choices. And just like the squirrel, he would be ready when winter came.

42.

REDUCING JOB LOSS STRESS

In Mumbai, amid the chaos of rising rents, job insecurities, and inflation, Kris found himself drowning in financial stress. Losing his job had amplified his worries, and each passing day brought mounting unpaid bills and growing anxiety. Sleepless nights were filled with thoughts of failure, his confidence eroding under the weight of constant negativity.

On a friend's advice, Kris met a Stress Support Guide whose words struck a chord: "Fear, anxiety, negativity, and stress are natural reactions to threats — they are animals in you responding. But stress won't solve your problems. To overcome this, be human. Be rational, use your intelligence."

Kris decided to face his situation head-on. He accepted that the job loss wasn't his fault and stopped blaming himself. Instead of dwelling on frustration, he focused on solutions. He reviewed his finances, tracked every expense, cut unnecessary spending, and extended his financial runway.

Determined, Kris shared his journey on LinkedIn. To his surprise, many people resonated with his story and reached out with support. A senior industrialist, impressed by his resilience, connected him with his HR department, leading to a great job opportunity.

Kris realized that setbacks weren't failures — they were stepping-stones to a new beginning.

43.

UNLOCKING THE GOLDEN HANDCUFFS

Jay, a 45-year-old senior executive, had everything — a high salary, luxury perks, and stock options. But he felt trapped in the golden handcuffs. The endless meetings, late-night emails, and pressure to perform drained him. He dreaded Mondays and envied those with the freedom to choose their work.

One night, staring at his laptop past midnight, he asked himself, *what's the worst that could happen if I quit?* Fear gripped him — losing financial security, lifestyle changes, judgment from peers. But another thought followed: *What's the worst if I stay?* His health was suffering, his relationships were strained, and he had no time for what truly mattered.

Jay began simplifying — cutting unnecessary expenses, investing wisely, and up skilling. He joined "Stress Support Guides," something he deeply cared about. Within months, he built a side practice, coaching and guiding professionals like himself.

When his bonus arrived, instead of feeling tied down again, he used it as his escape fund. With confidence, he resigned—stepping into a life he designed on his own terms.

A year later, he was coaching stressed executives—not as a trapped corporate leader, but as a free man.

The golden handcuffs had finally unlocked.

44.

STOICISM AND INDIFFERENCE: A SHIELD AGAINST STRESS

In a UK survey, most people reported stress due to job pressure, financial difficulties, health concerns, and relationship issues. These stressors often feed into each other — job stress creates financial pressure, which then leads to health and relationship problems. This is the stress spiral. But the real issue isn't the problem itself — it's our response to it.

Your brain interprets emotional reactions like fear, resistance, or frustration as signs of danger. This triggers the stress response — fight or flight. However, if you choose a Stoic or indifferent attitude, you break this loop. Suppose you face unrealistic deadlines, heavy workloads, or uncertainty. Instead of reacting emotionally, you consciously accept the situation. You see it not as a threat, but as a challenge to your inner strength — a test of your human spirit.

When you stop sending danger signals to your brain, the stress response calms down. You may still be physically tired, but mentally, you remain clear and stable. Most modern health and relationship issues are deeply linked to chronic stress. By refusing to get emotionally involved with every external trigger, you reduce unnecessary suffering. A Stoic mindset allows you to respond wisely, stay balanced, and find practical solutions — even in chaos.

45.

ADVICE ON REDUCING DEBT

Kevin sat across from Guru, eyes clouded with anxiety. "I've maxed out two credit cards, my loan repayments eat up half my salary. I feel like I'm drowning."

Guru smiled gently. "Debt is like carrying a heavy backpack uphill. First, stop adding more weight. Pause all non-essential spending. Use cash or UPI."

"Second," Guru continued, "list all your debts — amounts, interest rates — and prioritize. Either repay the loan with the highest interest first or pay off the smallest one to build momentum."

Kevin scribbled notes, finally seeing a road map.

"Third," Guru said, "negotiate. Call your banks. Ask for lower interest rates or revised EMIs. Many people don't ask — but many banks say yes."

"And what if I still struggle?" Kevin asked.

"Then increase your income — take up part-time gigs, freelancing, or sell unused items. Every extra rupee should go toward repayment. Debt is not just a financial burden; it's an emotional weight. Each rupee you repay is reclaiming your peace. Be patient. Be consistent. Soon, the weight will be off — and your mind will be free to explore more possibilities and opportunities."

46.

JOB INSECURITY

Vishy, a 32-year-old marketing executive, felt deeply anxious. Trump had launched a trade war. Layoff rumors were swirling, and his mind was consumed with one question: *What if I lose my job?* He couldn't focus, his sleep suffered, and stress drained his energy.

He consulted a Stress Support Guide, who told him, "Anxiety doesn't secure a job — skills and mindset do." The guide advised Vishy to list his strengths, update his resume, and reach out to organizations where he could add value. "Uncertainty is scary, but preparation gives you control."

Inspired, Vishy took action. He enrolled in an online course on digital marketing, expanded his LinkedIn network, and gradually explored freelance projects.

A month later, his company announced layoffs — but Vishy wasn't paralyzed by fear anymore. Even though he lost his job, he already had interview calls lined up.

Within weeks, Vishy secured a better role. He realized that stress wasn't the enemy — his reaction to it was. Instead of fearing uncertainty, he learned to prepare for it. That mindset made all the difference.

47.

THE POWER OF TRUTH AND ACTION

Mr. Kripal Singh Bedi, once the India Head of a multinational hotel group, faced a crushing blow during COVID. He was sacked on unfounded allegations, pending investigation, and left unpaid. His family lived lavishly—his wife a socialite, his son chasing big dreams, and his daughter obsessed with reels and designer clothes. For months, he pretended to be busy, maxed out credit cards, and maintained a false front. The façade crumbled when collection agents began hounding him.

One day, he met Guru, who told him, “Losing a job isn’t shameful — pretending is.” Encouraged, Kripal had a raw, honest conversation with his family. Tears flowed, but so did healing. Without asking, money started pouring in from extended family. His brother-in-law wired $5,000 from Canada. His wife gave up her fake lifestyle and started a home-cooked meal business. His son began working in PPE supply. His daughter became an influencer and monetized her channel.

Kripal partnered with his former head chef and launched a cloud kitchen selling biryani. Today, he’s a major player in the Indian food industry. Their IPO was oversubscribed 5X. His journey turned not because of luck — but because he stopped pretending, embraced honesty, and took action.

48.

FROM STRESS TO SPICE: A NEW BEGINNING

Rehan and Rani, both 31, were drowning in financial stress. Despite their corporate jobs, EMIs, rising rent, and endless bills, late nights left them exhausted. Their dream of a peaceful life felt distant — until one night, while staring at their bank statements, Rani whispered, “What if we just left?”

A month later, they moved to Himachal, using their savings to rent a small home in a spice-growing village. Life slowed down — no traffic, no boss, just crisp mountain air. Inspired by the rich organic spices around them, they launched an online business, supplying fresh turmeric, cardamom, and cinnamon to city dwellers craving purity.

Challenges came — slow sales, tricky logistics — but they persisted. Rani handled marketing; Rehan built partnerships with local farmers. Soon, orders grew, and so did their peace. Mornings were for hiking, evenings for hand-packing orders. One evening, as they sipped chai by a misty valley, Rehan smiled, “We earn less, but we live more.”

They had traded financial stress for meaningful work, anxiety for purpose. Not rich in money — but rich in life. And that was enough.

49.

HOW AMITABH BACHCHAN OVERCAME A CRISIS

Amitabh Bachchan faced a severe financial crisis when his company ABCL Ltd. defaulted on loans. As the guarantor, he had to repay creditors from his personal funds. His accounts were depleted, his assets — including his house — were attached by banks, and he had no work. However, instead of succumbing to stress or blaming others, he focused on solutions.

He maintained self-control and accepted the reality of his situation. He didn't dwell on "Why me?" but asked, "What can I do?" Since big film production houses weren't offering work, he turned to television and created an opportunity by hosting a show. Rather than waiting for producers, he sought them out and asked for work.

Regarding his debts, he personally analyzed the problems and dealt with them instead of relying solely on legal or financial advisors. He negotiated fairly, requesting the removal of penalties and compound interest to reach just settlements. He also cut down on personal expenses and made tough decisions, including asking his son to return from Boston University to reduce costs and contribute financially.

Throughout this period, he followed a disciplined lifestyle — exercising, meditating, expressing gratitude, seeking support from family and friends, and avoiding unhealthy coping mechanisms. He maintained a steady routine, slept early, stayed focused, and took one day at a time.

50.

KEVIN'S TURNING POINT

Kevin stared at his phone — another rejection email. He had lost his job two months ago, had no savings, and bills were piling up. Rent was due, groceries were running low, and each passing day felt heavier.

At first, panic consumed him — sleepless nights, constant worry, and endless job searches. But then, he paused. *"Stress won't solve this. What can I control?"*

He created a structured routine — mornings for job applications, afternoons for learning new skills, and evenings for walks. To calm his racing mind, he practiced deep breathing — four counts in, four counts out — whenever anxiety hit. Instead of drowning in negative thoughts, he began writing down three things he was grateful for each day, shifting his focus from scarcity to possibility and hope. He also started journaling his worries, which made them feel less overwhelming. Meditation helped him stay present and reduced his habit of overthinking the future.

One day, a friend asked him to help make a YouTube video. Kevin enjoyed framing the shot, setting up lights, and capturing audio. He picked up editing very quickly and contributed creatively, helping make excellent content that gained attention.

Encouraged by this, he and his friend rented a small space in Andheri, Mumbai, and started a studio that helped creators make videos. Slowly, they expanded, creating videos for corporate clients. Today, they are among the most successful digital content creators in Mumbai.

51.

REDUCING STRESS IN RELATIONSHIPS

Amit and Priya had been married for five years, but lately, their relationship felt strained. Financial stress was mounting, and small disagreements often turned into heated arguments. Priya felt Amit didn't understand her worries, while Amit thought Priya expected too much.

One evening, after another fight, they decided to sit down and talk. They realized their lack of communication was fueling their stress. Amit began sharing his financial concerns, and Priya, instead of blaming him, listened. She acknowledged his efforts, and together, they worked on a budget.

They also agreed to be a little blind to each other's faults and deaf to unnecessary complaints. Instead of focusing on flaws, they appreciated small gestures — a morning coffee, a kind word. They set aside time for weekend walks, shared hobbies, and little surprises.

Physical affection and laughter returned. They reminded themselves that a relationship is built on shared moments, not just coexistence. They communicated openly, forgave quickly, and avoided blame. When conflicts arose, they resolved them before they became mountains. For deeper issues, they sought counseling, which further strengthened their bond.

Their relationship flourished — not because life became easier, but because they chose to invest in each other.

52.

LOVE REKINDLED

Raj and Raashi had been married for six years. Their once passionate love had faded into exhaustion. Raashi was consumed with caring for their three-year-old son, Rohan. Raj, burdened by work, felt like nothing more than a provider. Their conversations had devolved into complaints — Raashi accused him of being absent, while Raj resented feeling neglected.

Arguments became frequent, sharp words replacing soft whispers. One evening, after a heated fight, Raashi broke down. "I miss us," she admitted, tears streaming. Raj sighed, *"Me too... but I feel invisible."* That night, instead of blaming each other, they truly talked.

They decided to share responsibilities differently. Raj took on bedtime routines, cherishing Rohan's giggles. Raashi, making an effort, planned a surprise date night. Slowly, they found moments of laughter again—stealing kisses in the kitchen, watching movies after Rohan slept.

One evening, as Raj hugged Raashi from behind, she smiled. *"We forgot we were a team."* He nodded, holding her closer. Their love wasn't lost — it had just needed attention, like a fire needing fuel. Through patience, effort, and love, they didn't just stay together — they rediscovered each other.

53.

ARYAN AND NAINA

Aryan and Naina had once been madly in love. But over the years, their differences evolved into constant battles. Aryan — practical and reserved — struggled to express his emotions, while Naina — sensitive and expressive — felt unheard. Their fights grew colder, their silences more oppressive. Their five-year-old daughter Aaina watched in confusion as her parents drifted apart.

One evening, as Aryan packed his bags, Aaina clung to him, tears streaming down her face. "Papa, will you still love me if you leave?" That question shattered Aryan's heart. That night, he and Naina sat together for the first time in months — raw and vulnerable.

"I feel like I'm never enough for you," Naina whispered.

"I feel like you don't see how hard I try," Aryan admitted.

For the first time, they truly listened. They realized their love hadn't faded—it was buried under ego and unspoken words. They sought counseling, learned to communicate, and prioritized moments of togetherness. It wasn't easy, but love, when nurtured, has the power to heal.

Months later, Aaina struggled to squeeze in between her parents as they danced in the living room — no longer strangers, but partners again. Their love story wasn't perfect, but it was real — and that was enough.

54.

THE TRUTH HAT TECHNIQUE: A MARRIAGE SAVER

Ms. D'Souza's marriage was deteriorating into a cycle of criticism and emotional distance. Her husband sulked, complained, and drank late into the night. Conversations devolved into arguments. Love felt increasingly distant.

On a short getaway to Goa, she brought a simple yet powerful idea — a hat. Handing it to her husband, she said, "This is the Truth Hat. When we wear it, we must share our deepest concerns about our marriage without fear. No judgment, no anger — just honesty."

He hesitated but agreed. As he wore the hat, he revealed his frustrations — the pressures, unmet expectations, and how he felt unappreciated. When it was her turn, she spoke about her loneliness, his absence, and how his drinking hurt her. Some truths were painful, some were easy to fix, and some had no solutions — but they needed to be heard.

It wasn't easy, but the exercise rekindled their lost connection. That night, they held each other a little longer. The Truth Hat didn't just expose wounds — it helped them heal. They left Goa not just as a couple, but as partners ready to rebuild their love, understanding, and respect.

Sometimes, all a marriage needs is a safe space for truth.

55.

BREAKING FREE TOGETHER

Khushi and Shaan's love story had blossomed in college. But after marriage, it turned into constant battle. Living in a joint family, Khushi faced daily disapproval. Shaan's grandmother had never accepted her. His parents made her quit her job, confining her to domestic chores she despised.

The house felt like a prison – snide remarks, subtle taunts, and an overbearing matriarch chipped away at Khushi's spirit. She felt high – strung, invisible, and trapped in a life she hadn't chosen.

One evening, after a painful outburst, Shaan sat quietly with Khushi. He saw her tears – not of anger, but exhaustion. He said, "This is not the life we dreamed of. Let's make a change- together.

They met Guru, who told them, "Marriage is a team. If one is drowning, the other must hold them up. Be SRI – sensible, rational, and intelligent. Create space to breathe, to grow, and to live with dignity.

With courage, they moved into a small apartment. Khushi restarted her career. Shaan supported her fully. The distance from judgement brought them closer to each other. Khushi smiled again – not because life was perfect, but because they chose each other every day. Together, they broke free, built their own peaceful world.

56.

NAVIGATING STRESS IN MARRIAGE

Guru was addressing a group of newly married couples.

"Marriage is a beautiful journey — but it comes with challenges. Remember, you both come from different backgrounds and upbringings. Early on, adjusting to each other's habits and expectations can feel overwhelming. Open communication is key—talk about feelings without blame. Set healthy boundaries with extended family to maintain your space."

"As careers grow, balancing work and marriage becomes challenging. Support each other's ambitions, celebrate wins together, and prioritize quality time. Don't let work stress spill into your relationship — create a 'stress-free zone' at home."

"Financial stress often creeps in. Budget together, plan expenses, and be transparent about money. Create an emergency fund — because sometimes, income may stop, but expenses won't."

"When children arrive, the family dynamic shifts dramatically. Parenting is physically and emotionally exhausting. Personal time shrinks. Share responsibilities and deliberately schedule couple time to keep the romantic spark alive."

"Mid-life challenges — aging parents, career changes, or health concerns — can strain a marriage. Approach them as a team, leaning on each other's strengths. Practice daily gratitude. Focus on what's working, not what's missing?"

"No marriage is perfect — nurture your bond."

57.

COUPLE CHALLENGES

Anup and Meera, a millennial couple, were drowning in stress. Anup's tech job was unstable, and Meera's marketing role demanded 12–hour days and constant travel. Their conversations revolved around EMIs, expenses and exhaustion.

One night after a heated argument, Meera broke down. "I can't live like this," she whispered. Her tears shook Anup. Holding her hand, he said, "We have to stop living like we're constantly drowning."

They met Guru, who introduced them to the *SRI Approach* – Be **Sensible, Rational,** and **Intelligent** in every decision. Guru helped them reassess their life – not just their stress. They cut unnecessary expenses, moved to a smaller flat closer to Meera's office and created a shared saving plan to build one-year emergency fund. Anup explored up skilling in cyber security – an emerging more stable field – and took evening classes. Meera moved to cosmetic and beauty start up on verge of getting Series A funding, in addition to higher salary, city-based work, she also got ESOP.

They scheduled weekly "life meetings" to review finances, chores and emotions – no blame, just solutions. Slowly life became lighter. They didn't just manage stress – they redesigned their life. Guru smiled, "When you live consciously and make long term choices together, love becomes source of strength – not stress.

58.

THE FAVOR TRAP.

Neha's colleague Raj was always too friendly. "Hey, can you help me with this slide. You're great at it." She'd help and Raj would take credit in meetings. When she hinted at it, he brushed it off "Come on, we're a team. Don't be transactional." She felt guilty for even doubting his intentions.

Then one weekend, she stayed late helping him polish a pitch. On Monday, Raj presented it as his solo effort. Neha felt used. But instead of reacting emotionally, she paused – and activated **SRI approach**.

She was **Sensible**: "He's not a friend. He is using praise and guilt to control me." She was **Rational**: "This is a pattern. I must break it with clarity." She was Intelligent: She stopped doing quiet favors. She ensured her contributions were documented and visible. She didn't explode. She set **boundaries** – with calm strength. The next time Raj asked for "a small favour," She smiled, "Sorry, I have my own deliverables." No guilt, no anger. Just quiet power.

Raj didn't protest. He simply turned to Sonam with same line: "Hey, can you help me with a slide. Neha smiled. She had learned a key truth: *Manipulations only works on those who doubt their right to say no.*

59.

SIA'S SECOND CHANCE

Sia had married for love, ignoring warnings from family and friends. But love soon turned into control. Her husband mocked her dreams, dismissed her efforts, and made her feel small.

With their beautiful daughter in her arms, Sia endured — believing things would change.

Her wings felt clipped — trapped between nurturing responsibilities and financial dependence. But one night, as she watched her daughter sleep, a painful truth struck her:

She didn't want her little one to grow up seeing love as sacrifice — or fearing relationships.

Determined, Sia started small. She took online courses at night, learned digital marketing, and slowly built her freelance work. Every penny she earned became her ticket to freedom.

Months turned into a year — she secured steady clients, saved enough, and found the courage she had lost.

One day, with trembling hands but an unshakeable heart, she walked away. Not just from her marriage — but from fear.

Sitting in her small, rented apartment, her daughter playing beside her, Sia smiled.

She wasn't broken; she was rebuilding.

She was free.

60.

DIVORCE – RITA'S NEW BEGINNING

Rita held the divorce paper, hands shaking. Her marriage had long been battlefield – sharp words, emotional wounds, silent sobs in the dark. Now alone with Aarav, her six-year-old autistic son, fear gripped her. No stable job, no real support. "How will you manage?" fear whispered.

That night Aarav had a meltdown. As she held him, shielding him from his storm, a truth hit her – she too was breaking inside but no one was holding her. She decided to hold herself. She reached out – to an autism NGO, to women help group. She updated her resume, brushed up her LinkedIn profile, and stepped into legal battle, each insult strengthening her spine.

Then came hope. One evening, her mentor brought along a dignified man from a corporate group. "We run *Second Innings – a program to help women rebuild their lives,"* he said. A job, a chance, a future. One by one things were falling into place.

Later that night, Aarav hugged her tightly whispering, "Happy Mamma." She didn't have all the answers yet, but for the first time in years, the weight on her chest felt lighter. Rita wasn't just surviving anymore. She was beginning. A new life. A stronger self. Her second innings had just begun.

61.

TAKING CARE OF ELDERS-PRIYA'S STORY.

Priya's days blurred into a routine of sacrifice – caring for her bedridden mother-in-law, her ailing mother, her school-going children, and a husband who barely noticed. Nights were sleepless, meals skipped, her body aching, spirit drained. One evening while lifting a pot of boiling dal, a wave of dizziness swept over her. The doctor's verdict was blunt- "Your blood pressure is dangerously high. If you collapse, who will hold the fort?"

That night, tears soaked her pillow. By morning, resolve replaced silence. She sat Shridhar, her indifferent husband. "They are your parents too," she said, voice trembling but firm. He looked at her - deeply looked - for the first time in months. The fatigue in her eyes struck him. Shridhar agreed to hire a full-time attendant. Her brother stepped in to take care of their mother.

Small changes began. A part-time cook arrived. Priya joined a online yoga class. She found a support group that visited lonely elders – offering the same care she craved. Her daughter quietly began helping more at home.

Weeks later, the doctor smiled. "Normal pressure." Priya smiled too. She had always carried everyone. She just didn't know it was ok to ask someone to hold her, too.

62.

SINGLE DIVORCED PARENT

Guru was advising a single parent:

"Being a single parent, facing financial challenges and social disapproval, can feel overwhelming. But you are stronger than you realize.

First, prioritize your child's emotional well-being over material comforts. Children need love, attention, and security more than expensive things. Create simple routines, share quality time, and be emotionally present."

Financially, focus on small, steady steps: budget wisely, seek community resources, and don't hesitate to ask for help from trustworthy people or organizations. Avoid comparing your life to others — your journey is unique and valuable.

Social disapproval can be painful but remember: people's opinions do not define you. Surround yourself with supportive friends — even if it's just a few — and limit time with those who judge. Practice self-care through moments of rest, gratitude, or small activities you enjoy. Talk kindly to yourself — you are doing your best.

Most importantly, let your child feel loved, heard, and accepted. Your resilience will teach them strength, empathy, and courage. Stress will come, but it doesn't have to stay.

One day at a time — with small acts of love and care — you can create a nurturing space for both you and your child to thrive.

63.

THE DINNER TABLE TRUCE

Ronny dreaded family dinners. Every meeting turned into a battlefield – his father criticized his job choices, his mother compared him to his "perfect" cousin, and his younger sister stayed silent, trying to avoid the tension.

Many times, Ronny would just get up and leave when arguments erupted. But this time, he decided to stay and speak his heart. As another argument brewed, Ronny snapped:

"Why do I always feel like I'm not enough?"
"I get stressed just thinking about these dinners." His voice cracked. The table fell silent.

His mother hesitated, and then sighed. **"We just want the best for you."**

"By making me feel like a failure?" Ronny's eyes burned.

His father intervened, **"Ronny, we are scared. The world is tough. We push you because we worry."**

"But you're not helping me," Ronny replied. **"I'm anxious all the time. I can't sleep. I feel depressed. Please don't push me into a breakdown – or worse, addiction."**

That night, they set new rules: no criticism, more listening, more support.

The first few weeks were awkward, but over time, the fighting lessened. Dinner slowly became a place of understanding.

64.

ADOLESCENCE IMPACT

When Aryan turned 14, his parents noticed a shift — he was distant, irritable, and glued to his phone. They worried, often scolding him, thinking he was just being rebellious. But one evening, they attended a stress-reduction session with Guru.

Guru explained, "Adolescence is a stormy bridge between childhood and adulthood. Hormonal changes can cause mood swings. Teens crave independence but still need guidance. It's confusing for them — and for you."

Aryan's parents sighed in relief. Guru continued, "Instead of reacting with fear or anger, respond sensibly, rationally, intelligently. Ask, don't accuse. Listen more, advise less."

Turning to Aryan, he said, "Son, it may help if you share what's going on in your mind." Aryan hesitated, then admitted he felt pressured to succeed, to fit in with friends, and wasn't sure who he was becoming.

Guru smiled gently. "That's completely normal. Most adolescents go through this phase. Remember, what is needed is not perfection — but presence. Your parents love you, even if they don't always understand you."

Aryan's mother teared up. His father nodded silently. That evening, they didn't fight — they talked.

Adolescence isn't a problem to fix — it's a transition to navigate, together. With understanding, patience, and connection, families can turn conflict into closeness. Guru reminded them, "This too shall pass. But how you respond can shape who they become."

65.

THE WEIGHT OF A GRUDGE

Ashish held a grudge against his ex-boss for years. After being unfairly fired, waves of anger surged through him every time he thought about it. He would replay the incident in his mind, imagining comebacks he never delivered. But while his ex-boss had moved on, Ashish remained stuck, reliving his pain.

One day, Guru asked him, "How does holding on to this anger help you?"

Ashish realized it didn't. It only triggered stress, ruined his mood, and drained his energy. His ex-boss wasn't suffering — Ashish was.

Forgiving doesn't mean justifying what happened; it means freeing ourselves from the mental burden. A grudge is like carrying a heavy backpack — letting go lightens our emotional load. Forgetting doesn't mean erasing the past but choosing not to let it control our present.

When Ashish decided to let go, he felt an unexpected peace. His mind, once trapped in resentment, found space for better things — new opportunities, relationships, and happiness.

Letting go isn't for the other person — it's for us. It's how we reclaim our peace, reduce stress, and move forward without unnecessary emotional baggage. Why stay in prison when you hold the key to freedom?

66.

MENOPAUSE

Guru was speaking to a group of women. "Dear sisters, menopause is not the end — it's a new beginning. But yes, it comes with challenges: hormonal changes, mood swings, sleep issues, body changes, and a mind that sometimes feels overwhelmed. The stress is real. But let's pause and be sensible."

"You are not who you were at 30," he continued. "And that's not a loss — it's a shift. Accepting this shift reduces inner resistance."

"Be rational — your body is changing, and so is your inner wisdom. Journal your feelings. Talk. Share. Walk. Meditate. Be mindful. This reflection helps you understand yourself deeply, without judgment."

"Be intelligent — connect with joyful people, don't isolate. Ladies-only tours to explore the world are great. Enjoy sisterhood. Integrate nourishing habits. Do yoga. Eat more mindfully. Sleep without screens. Rediscover reading. Enjoy life."

Stress after menopause isn't a flaw — it's a signal. A call to care more, not less, for yourself. Let this be your mantra: *'I am not less; I am becoming more in new ways.'*

You have weathered storms before. You will rise again — but this time, softer, steadier, stronger.

The group nodded — some with tears, others with smiles — but all feeling a little lighter.

67.

LATE BLOOMER

At 35, Rehan's life felt like a failure. He drifted between jobs, confidence shattered, shame rising. His friends had careers, families, homes. He had excuses and disappointment. When young interns mockingly called him "grandfather," he laughed outwardly – but crumbled inside.

His father, heartbroken, met Guru. "Rehan was such an intelligent boy," he said, eyes moist." But he loses interest in everything." Rehan agreed to meet Guru who asked him one question: "What would you do with all your heart - even if no one paid you?" Rehan hesitated, then whispered, "Music. I used to write songs, compose – but who wants that?" Guru smiled, "Start with one. Not for the world – for you. Rehan isn't lost. He just hasn't found his song."

Rehan began writing again. He composed late into the night, pouring his emotions into melodies. One day, he recorded a song for his mother and uploaded it to YouTube. The lyrics – raw, honest, aching – touched millions. His story became theirs. Within two years, Rehan was a globally loved song writer and singer.

Backstage in London, he called his parents. "Thanks for believing in me - even when I had lost belief in self." Guru once said *"A seed buried in darkness isn't dead – it's preparing to bloom."* Rehan bloomed – and became a forest of hope.

68.

YOU DON'T HAVE TO FACE IT ALONE

Keerat Kaur's life had been defined by love, sacrifice, and resilience. But when she received the news that her only son had fallen in combat during the Kargil War, her world shattered. Just a few years earlier, he had donned the Army uniform with pride — just like his father, who had died a war hero in the 1971 Bangladesh Liberation War. Now, she was alone. The grief was unbearable; an emptiness consumed her.

Anna D'sa, a stress support guide, visited her. Recognizing Keerat's silent suffering, Anna gently urged her to seek therapy.

"Depression is like a dark fog," she said. "But you don't have to face it alone."

They began taking long walks, and Keerat slowly opened Up — her pain finding a voice.

One day, Anna took her to a dog adoption meet up. Amidst the crowd, a small, skinny puppy with big, hopeful eyes caught Keerat's attention. When she gazed into those eyes, she saw resilience — a reflection of her own heart. At that moment, she decided to adopt him, naming him *Zorawar*, meaning "brave."

Caring for Zorawar gave her a new purpose. His playful energy filled the void in her heart. And with every wag of his tail, her grief felt a little lighter.

69.

THE POWER OF CONNECTION

Aaron had always been a lone warrior. He believed dealing with stress was a personal battle. Long hours at work, relentless pressure, and self-doubt had become his norm. He often felt exhausted, but he kept pushing — until one evening, his body gave in. A panic attack left him gasping for breath.

That night, he called Guru. Aaron shared his struggles. Instead of judgment, he found warmth. Guru listened, reassured him, and invited him to the Stress Busters meet up.

Listening to stories of sharing and caring, Aaron felt lighter. Then came the singing, playing, dancing, and laughing — it made him feel good. He met a calm, tranquil person who gently asked if he was comfortable sharing what was bothering him. Aaron felt an instant trust and opened up. So did others. He realized he wasn't alone — everyone had their battles. And together, they found strength.

With time, these connections became his anchor. Venting to friends, seeking advice from mentors, and simply knowing someone had his back made him more resilient. His stress levels dropped, his mind felt clearer, and for the first time in years, he felt truly supported.

Stress had made him believe he was alone. But connection reminded him he never was.

70.

THE EMPTY BALCONY

Early evening, Mr. Rao sat alone on his balcony, watching the world go by. The calls from his son were polite but rushed, and the silence that followed felt heavier with each passing day.

One evening, Guru visited the senior center and gently asked, “Would you like to share your journey with those who feel lost?”

Mr. Rao looked up, surprised. Guru continued, “We are forming a Stress Support Group. People — especially the young — are drowning in confusion, pressure, and loneliness. Your wisdom could be their lighthouse.”

Reluctantly, he attended. At first, he just listened. But when a young man spoke of losing direction after his father’s death, something stirred. Mr. Rao shared his own loss, his struggles with aging, and how silence had almost swallowed him.

Weeks passed. Mr. Rao became a mentor to a few young citizens. His calm voice, seasoned by life, offered them comfort. He was soon invited to speak at the Rotary, Lions, and Senior Citizens Clubs, sharing his challenges, experiences, and learnings. There was peace in guiding others.

“I thought I had nothing left,” he said at one gathering, “but life gave me a second calling — helping others find their way.”

His balcony didn’t change. But Mr. Rao did.
Purpose replaced loneliness. He began to live again.

71.

LIFE IS LIKE A GAME OF CRICKET

Guru stood before the young IPL players and said, "Life is a unique game of cricket. The universe is the bowler — and it bowls all kinds of deliveries: bouncers of sudden stress, yorkers of unexpected pressure, googlies of confusion, and full tosses of joy. You don't control the ball; you play what comes."

He paused, letting the words sink in. "Some overs will be full of runs — success, celebration, flow. Some will be maidens — no progress, only patience. You'll hit sixes, get caught, get run out or even fall injured. But remember, you're not out until the final ball. The crowd will cheer when you succeed and mock when you fail. But a real player? He isn't distracted by the noise."

"A great cricketer plays for the love of the game. He remains calm under pressure, adapts his strategy, watches the bowler, learns, and grows. He doesn't let anger or fear break his focus. He knows that when the situation isn't as he would like, there will be negative thoughts and emotions. But like any good cricketer, he understands that to win, you need, not just talent, skill, focus, and determination, but also mental strength to face difficult balls with indifference."

So too in life — play the ball as it comes.
Stay present. Evolve your game.
The goal isn't just to win, but to play with awareness, passion, and grace.

72.

THE SPOTLIGHT FADES

Amit sat alone in his dimly lit bungalow, the silence louder than the applause he once knew. Three back-to-back flops. Scripts stopped coming. His phone, once buzzing with offers, now lay cold and still. Anxiety gripped his chest like a vice.

"Was I just a phase? A lucky face in a lucky role?"
The mirror across the room showed not a star, but a middle-aged man unraveling.

His mind replayed critics' harsh words, fans' fading admiration, and the haunting emptiness of having no project in hand. He stopped going out. Avoided calls. Spent his time brooding, anxious, and afraid.

One night, scrolling mindlessly, he came across a short video of Guru:
"When nothing is working outside, control what is working inside. Getting anxious, losing confidence in yourself is not going to help. There is a problem — what are you doing about it? Work out solutions."

Something in those words cracked through his fog. He picked up the phone and spoke to his agent about that television role. He discussed how, if not the hero, he could still portray the hero's father — a strong character. He also agreed to take up a voiceover project because it paid well, and he was short on money.

Getting worried, feeling anxious, getting stressed — none of it helps.
What might help is the question:
"What are you doing about it?"

73.

PROCRASTINATION

Rohan had a dream – to launch his own podcast. The idea lit him up inside. But every time he sat down to record the first episode, his mind pulled him away. *"I need a better mic,"* he told himself. Then it was, *"I need a better script.... Better voice..... better mood."* Days turned into weeks. The excitement faded into self - doubt.

Rohan wasn't lazy. He was stuck. The **animal brain** in him – the one wired for safety – was afraid. It whispered, *"What if it's not good enough? What if people laugh?"* So, it tricked him into delaying, disguising fear as preparation.

He spoke to Guru, who said "Perfection is often procrastination in disguise. Your higher self that is your discipline and determination should take lead to prevail over the animal in you." Guru offered simple steps.

1. **Start small** – Record a 2 – minute voice notes just for yourself.
2. **Set a deadline** – not for a perfect but for done.
3. **Break the fear** – Share one imperfect clip with a friend.
4. **Detach from outcome** – Focus on creation and not reaction.
5. **Reward action, not resul**t – Celebrate showing up, not just success.

Rohan followed through. His first episode wasn't perfect – but it was real. And that was enough to begin. *Sometimes progress begins when you stop waiting to feel ready – and simply start.*

74.

OVERTHINKING

Anna sat at her desk, staring at her phone. Her mind raced.

"Did I say something wrong at the client meeting? Why did my boss stare at me? Will my superiors think I'm incompetent?"

She sighed and scrolled through social media. Another friend was vacationing in Italy.
"Life sucks. Everybody's enjoying except me. I'm stuck."

Just then, her mentor, Sia, walked in and noticed Anna's tense face.

"Anna, what's on your mind?" Sia asked gently.

Anna hesitated, but then poured out her thoughts. Sia listened quietly, then picked up a coffee mug.

"Hold this," she said.

Anna took the mug. Then Sia handed her a phone, a file, a pen, and a notebook. Anna struggled to hold everything.

"Why are you giving me so much to hold?" Anna asked.

Sia smiled. "That's what you're doing to your mind—carrying too much at once."

Anna frowned. "But how do I stop overthinking?"

Sia took the coffee mug back. "Your mind will have automatic thoughts. Simplify — focus on what you can control." She took the phone. "Reflect — notice when your thoughts are draining you." Finally, she took the file. "Resolve — let go of what doesn't serve you."

75.

SLEEP

Roy struggled to sleep after learning that his company was cutting costs. Uncertainty and insecurity triggered anxious thoughts, affecting his concentration and leaving him fatigued. Seeking help, he met a Stress Support Guide, who advised him to manage his thoughts through journaling and self-reflection.

"Cross the bridge when you come to it," the guide reminded him.

Instead of fearing the worst, Roy needed to trust his ability to find solutions. Anxiety, after all, only harmed his health and made things harder.

To sleep better, the guide suggested settling worries before bedtime — resolving what could be handled and mentally releasing the rest. He encouraged disconnecting from screens an hour before bed, taking a warm bath, drinking a soothing cup of milk, and reading a calming book.

Sleep isn't instant; it requires a wind-down period. Going to bed at least 30 minutes early allowed thoughts to settle gradually. Meditation techniques like Yog Nidra further added relaxation.

By following these steps, Roy improved his sleep, felt more rested, and handled challenges with a clearer mind. Stress didn't disappear overnight, but with better sleep, he faced life with strength and clarity.

76.

THE VOICE IN HER HEAD

Savi stared at her screen, her heart racing. Another work email. Another mistake pointed out.

"I'm so stupid. I can't do anything right."

The words echoed in her mind, making her chest tighten.

She was preoccupied at home and burned the toast. *"I mess up everything."* Her friend canceled plans. *"No one really wants to be with me."* She glanced in the mirror. *"I've grown fat. I don't look good."*

Guru smiled when she shared this. "Stress isn't just about external pressure, Savi. It's also about the pressure we put on ourselves through our thoughts. Change your words, and you change your world."

That night, she wrote down her thoughts and rewrote them:
"I make mistakes, but I'm learning."
"People have their reasons; it's not always about me."
I am worthy, just as I am."

Guru explained, "Speak to yourself the way you would speak to your best friend. "Would you ever criticize your best friend, when they are feeling low. You wouldn't - so why are you criticizing yourself?"

Savi got the message. The real battle wasn't outside — it was inside. She was ready to change what she was saying to herself. Stress didn't vanish, but it loosened its grip.

77.

INTERNAL PRESSURE

On the sidelines of a seminar, the Mumbai sales manager asked Guru, "My boss doesn't shout at me... but I feel constant pressure. It's all inside me. How do I deal with that?" Guru smiled and pulled out a balloon from his pocket. "This is your life," he said, slowly blowing air into it. Expectations... comparison... needing to be better than others... fear of failure... target... appraisal... promotion... proving your worth..." With each word, he added more air, till the balloon was about to burst.

Finally, he stopped and held the balloon at eye level. "You see, your life isn't exploding from outside – it's inflating from within. *You're the one filling it with pressure."* The manager looked down thoughtfully.

Guru continued, "Now let's deflate it. Let go of the need to please everyone. Let go of comparing yourself. Let go of believing stress equals success. Take things one step at a time. Focus on doing, not proving. Pause when you feel full. Breathe. Reset. He slowly released air from the balloon until it softened. "This is still a balloon. It still holds shape – but now there's space inside."

Guru smiled, "Don't be your own pressure. Be your peace."

78.

BREAKING FREE FROM DOOM SCROLLING

Ayesha, a fashion designer, was glued to her phone. Night after night, she scrolled through Instagram's perfect lives. LinkedIn's career wins, and endless fashion shows on YouTube. She'd sleep past midnight, her mind racing, her confidence sinking.

One night, she stumbled upon an article about **dopamine addiction**– how social media hijacks the brain's reward system, feeding tiny hits of pleasure that keeps us scrolling... mindlessly. It hit her: *She wasn't relaxing – she was escaping, and the cost was her sleep and her peace.*

Determined to take control, Ayesha met Guru, who said," Your phone is not the enemy, your mind craving is. Let's reset your system. He gave her a 7-day **digital detox plan:**

- No phone for 1 hour after waking or before bed.
- Replace scrolling with journalling or reading.
- Keep apps off the home screen.
- Set 2 fixed times a day for social media.
- Go on dopamine fast – walk, cook, create, with no screens.
- Celebrate silence. Feel boredom. Reconnect with self.
- Reflect every night. Did I live today, or just scroll through it?

Within weeks, her sleep improved, her creativity returned. She didn't quit the online world – she reclaimed her place in. real one.

79.

SLEEP DEPRIVED STORM

Piyush was the star performer at his tech start-up – fast, sharp, and always on. Sleep felt like a waste of time. Caffeine, deadlines, and ambition became his fuel.

Then it started – forgotten passwords, chest tightness, snapping at colleagues, brain fog. He dismissed it all as a phase – until he blacked out during a major investor presentation. The doctor's verdict was clear: "You're severally sleep–deprived. Your body is rebelling. Those words struck him hard. That night, for the first time in years, Piyush asked himself – *What's the point of performance, if it costs me my health?*

He met Guru, who said, Success doesn't require self – destruction. Smart professionals manage energy, not just time."

Piyush made strategic changes: Set **firm boundaries:** no work calls post 9 PM. **Delegated non-critical tasks** to focus on high-impact decisions. Introduced **no-meeting zones** before 11 AM for deep work. Replaced late-night coding with **7 hours of sleep**. Scheduled short walks and unplugged breaks in his calendar. Measured success not just in KPI's but in clarity, calm, and consistency.

He didn't slow down his career. He sharpened it – with better thinking, stronger health and sustainable pace.

80.

THE FOGGY ROAD

Nikita, a 29-year-old graphic designer, often lay awake at night staring at the ceiling. Thoughts raced: *"Will AI replace graphic designing?" "What if I lose my job?" "Will Raj marry me?"*

The future felt like a foggy road — uncertain, full of invisible threats. She tried meditation, journaling, even overworking to silence the noise. But the relief was always temporary; nothing lasted.

One evening, she called Guru. He simply asked,
"Nikita, when you drive through fog, do you stop the car?"
She said, **"No, I just slow down and focus on the next few meters."**
Guru said, **"Exactly. Life is the same."**

That hit her. She had been trying to control the whole road when all she really needed was to stay present, take small steps, and trust that the way would reveal itself.

She shifted her approach: one day, one decision, one breath at a time. She replaced *"What if"* with *"What now?"*

Three months later, she didn't have all the answers—but she had peace. The fog was still there, but she no longer feared it.

81.

PURPOSE OF LIFE

One serene morning, Mr. Agrawal, a wealthy industrialist, asked Guru. "What is real purpose of life?"

Guru smiled and replied, "The purpose of life is to be *human.* Not just in body, but in thought, action, and spirit. All religions affirm that human birth is rare gift – granted to a soul ready to evolve. But look at what most people do – react like animals. They feel bad, get angry, anxious, and insecure and let stress ruin their body. This doesn't solve anything – it only leads to disease, high blood pressure, diabetes and heart conditions."

He continued, "The purpose of life is to *live fully* – with all its ups and downs. Problems are not punishments; they are opportunities to grow. Life must be lived on your terms – not in reaction, but with *awareness.* Choose to have happy thoughts, even in pain. Happiness isn't a reward, it's a choice.

Guru added, "The purpose is also to be *responsible.* Out of millions of souls, you were chosen to receive this life. Honour that. Be responsible to yourself, your family, your society and to humanity.

"And finally," Guru concluded. *"Be useful.* Life flourishes when we serve each other. That is how the human ecosystem thrives. To be human is to help."

82.

I DON'T KNOW WHAT TO DO

Harsh sat before the Guru, anxiety etched on his face. **"I lost my job because of the merger. I don't know what to do."**

Guru smiled,
"One of the best ways to figure that out is to find your *Ikigai* — the Japanese secret to a stress-free life. *Ikigai* is the sweet spot where passion, profession, vocation, and mission align. It's when what you love to do is also what people need, what they are willing to pay for, and what you're naturally good at."

Harsh frowned. "But how do I find it?"

"Think back—what excites you? What subjects did you score well in? What makes time fly? Your *Ikigai* is often hidden in those moments."

"Sachin Tendulkar, Roger Federer, Narendra Modi, Elon Musk, Amitabh Bachchan — think of any successful person. The most likely reason they thrive is because they have found their Ikigai. Once you find yours, work won't feel like a burden; it will become a source of energy and joy.

Find your *Ikigai*, and you'll never have to wonder what to do again."

83.

GRATITUDE

Guru was speaking to his trainees.
"The other day, I went to the dentist with a terrible toothache. He numbed my gums, treated the problem, and gave me medicine. There was some discomfort, but the pain eased, and I felt better. I walked out feeling grateful.

But then a thought struck me — what would a chimpanzee do with the same pain? No dentist. No medicine. Just helpless suffering.

Science tells us that 98% of our DNA is the same as chimpanzees. The 2% difference is the size of intellect part of the human brain. Human intellect is 3 times larger than chimpanzee intellect because humans used their intelligence to solve their problem. Why? Because we asked one powerful question: *What can I do about it?*

Threatened by predators, chimpanzees get stressed, fight, run, or freeze — and they still do. But early humans thought, *how can I protect myself?* They picked up stones. Built spears. Created fire. Every time humans faced a problem, they did get stressed — but they controlled their stress and used their intellect to solve it. That is how humanity progressed.

And yet, today, billions suffer in silence — angry, anxious, and their health affected. But they don't ask "In what way, I can solve my problem"

Gratitude is not just feeling thankful for blessings. It is being thankful for the gift of intellect — which, if used well, can help rid us of our problems and keep us truly blessed."

84.

A NEW BEGINNING

Krishnan had spent his life working tirelessly, but as he retired, fear gripped him. Would he still be relevant? What would he do with his time?

One evening, he met his old colleague Rakesh, who had reinvented himself after retirement.

"You've spent decades handling stress at work," Rakesh said. "Why not help others manage theirs?"

The idea stuck. Krishnan enrolled in a Stress Support Guide certification program. He learned counseling techniques, stress-reduction strategies, and public speaking. Energized, he started organizing Stress Buster Meetups for millennials — offering guidance through workshops, one-on-one counseling, and webinars.

Soon, startups invited him to motivate their teams. Colleges welcomed him to inspire students. His webinars attracted professionals struggling with burnout.

Krishnan, once fearful of retirement, now had a packed schedule — engaging, motivating, and making a real impact.

One evening, after a college seminar, a student approached him.

"Sir, your talk changed my perspective. I feel hopeful."

Krishnan smiled, realizing he had found his new purpose. Retirement hadn't ended his journey. It had given him a new one — one that was more fulfilling.

85.

COFFEE CUP REVELATION

Priti stared at her screen, dreading another day of emails, meetings, and drafting. Once excited by her law firm job, she now felt drained. Her shoulders ached, her sleep was broken, and even weekends didn't help her recover.

That morning, Ganpat Mama, the old peon, brought her coffee. With a gentle smile he said, "Busy again to get your own cup?" Something inside her cracked. I'm just... bored. Same work, every day. How do you do the same thing again and again?"

Mama sat quietly and showed her two photos from his wallet. "When the mill shut down, my family had nothing. This job – carrying files, cleaning, serving coffee – gave us dignity. That's my daughter. I got her married because of this job. And that's my son, studying computer science. This job gave him that chance."

He smiled, "When I see someone stressed, I bring them coffee. A pause. A smile. That's my reward. Gratitude, beta. Gratitude gives meaning.

Priti stared at her coffee. Something had shifted. The work hadn't changed, but her lens had. She wasn't stuck – she had simply stopped seeing the ***why***. That morning, her coffee didn't just energize her – it awakened her.

ADDRESS TO THE GRADUATING STUDENTS

Guru addressed the graduating students:

"As you step into the next phase of your lives, some of you will receive job offers, while others may not. But remember — your worth is not defined by an offer letter. The human ecosystem is complex, and often, there are no clear answers to 'why'. Rejection may trigger fear, anxiety, or stress. That's the animal in you reacting to uncertainty. But true success comes when you respond like a human—rationally, intelligently and with resilience. Stressing over setbacks won't help, but finding solutions will.

Success is built on service. You provide value to others, and in return, they reward you. In a world of nearly 8 billion connected people, your unique skills can make a difference. Those who thrive have found their *ikigai*—a passion that serves others and creates value. If you develop expertise in something people need, material success will follow.

There will be tough times, and the temptation to escape—through distractions, alcohol, or avoidance—may arise. But problems don't disappear when ignored. Face them with intelligence, patience, and resilience. No challenge is beyond your capacity to solve. Stand strong, stays human, and creates your own path."

87.

LIFE EXPLAINED TO YOUNG STUDENTS

Guru was explaining life to young students:

“Alright, imagine your body as a car on a journey called life, carrying precious goods: you’re dreams, your relationships, and your well-being. Sometimes, the road ahead will not be smooth — there will be disappointments, uncertainty, or even sudden storms of unexpected events. There are sensors in every car — your eyes, ears, sense of smell, and feelings are those sensors.

Now, imagine an ancient person sitting beside you, interpreting those signals. That ancient person once faced real dangers like tigers. It represents the fear-processing center in your brain, called the amygdala. It’s job is to activate stress if it senses danger—so you can fight or flee to save your life.

In modern times, there are no tigers, but we face pressures — job stress, financial worries, relationship issues. The ancient part of our brain cannot differentiate between real threats and modern stressors, so it reacts with the same intensity, causing your body to become agitated, tense, and restless — ready to fight or run.

This is where you, as the driver of the car, come in. You must reason and analyze what’s bothering the ancient person within you. Use your intellect to think clearly and map out solutions. We must learn to gently calm that inner voice, take control of the steering wheel, and use wisdom to navigate the rocky patches. Panicking won’t make the journey smoother — wise navigation will.”

88.

ANN DUNHAM

Few people know the story of Ann Dunham, the mother of Barack Obama, the 44th President of the United States. As a young student at the University of Hawaii, she fell in love with Barack Obama Sr., a Kenyan student. Their love brought Barack Jr. into the world, but heartbreak followed when his father returned to Kenya—where he had already been married—abandoning them.

Determined, Ann pursued her studies while raising her son. She later married an Indonesian student, Lolo Soetoro, and had a daughter, Maya. However, life in Indonesia didn't align with her vision. Choosing independence over convention, she returned to Hawaii as a single mother of two. Love took a back seat as her focus shifted to creating social impact.

Ann earned her PhD in anthropology and dedicated her life to microfinance — helping poor women in developing countries gain financial independence. Her work laid the foundation for some of the world's largest microfinance institutions. Her legacy lived on through her children —Barack, who became President of United States of America, and Maya, who pursued her PhD and continued their mother's mission.

Ann Dunham's life was not defined by heartbreak but by resilience, purpose, and the belief that one person can transform the world — starting with their own struggles.

89.

STRATEGIES TO REDUCE STRESS FOR MILLENNIALS

At Guru's workshop, millennials shared their greatest sources of stress, and he offered simple yet powerful strategies:

Financial Stability – Save before you spend. Build an emergency fund. Avoid credit card debt. Maintain a good credit score. Financial security brings peace of mind.

Workplace Stress – Set boundaries; work should stay at work. Prioritize self-care: exercise, meditate, and breathe. If your workplace is toxic, consider a shift—your well-being matters more than a paycheck.

Mental Health – Lean on family, friends, or support groups. Accept uncertainty—it's part of life. Journal your thoughts. Cut down on social media; comparison is the thief of joy.

Relationship Challenges – Communicate openly. Respect and expect respect. Let go of unrealistic expectations — no relationship is perfect; it evolves with time.

Social Pressure – Life isn't a race. Follow your own timeline, not societies. Choose growth over competition, happiness over perfection.

Health and Wellness – Move daily, even if it's just a 10-minute walk. Take breaks—five-minute meditation works wonders. Eat well, stay hydrated, and avoid substances that drain you.

Tech Overload – Stay updated but set limits. Don't be a slave to screens. Schedule digital detoxes—your mind will thank you.

90.

MOKSHA AND NIRVANA

Guru was addressing students of philosophy.

"My dear students, in Eastern philosophy, *Moksha* and *Nirvana* are often seen as liberation from the cycle of birth and death — a release from suffering and a union with ultimate truth. But let me offer you a reflection: What if that liberation, that bliss, is not a distant goal after death, but a lived reality here and now?

Look around — no other species is as blessed as humanity. We have food, shelter, families, healthcare, education, art, music, freedom—and above all, choice. We can choose to serve one another, to create a self-sustaining world filled with comfort, safety, and joy.

You can choose happiness without a reason. You can choose not to suffer by changing your thoughts. Just like that, stress can fade and peace can arise — not from external situations, but from within.

Moksha and *Nirvana* are not rewards for the afterlife, but states of being — available now.

Sing. Dance. Laugh. Play. Serve. Choose to experience bliss — not someday, but today — by choosing the right thoughts. That, my dear ones, is true liberation. That is *Moksha*. That is *Nirvana*. Not in the heavens above, but in the heart awakened to joy."

91.

NATHU KAKA'S REVENGE

As I stepped into a garment shop at Shivaji Park, a trembling hand stopped me. It was Nathu Kaka — his face red with anger, his body shaking—not from age, but from betrayal.

For thirty years, he had served this shop with loyalty, not just as an employee but as family. The owner, a distant relative, had trusted him completely. But after the owner passed away, his son took over and dismissed Nathu Kaka, deeming him too old and too sickly.

"I gave my life to this place," he muttered, his voice thick with pain. "Now they throw me out like I am nothing."

I placed a hand on his shoulder. "Nathu Kaka, you can be angry, stressed, and sick — or you can use your wisdom. The pain is yours, but so is the power to change."

Something clicked. He calmed down and started exploring options. A nearby shopkeeper — ready to retire but reluctant to shut down his family business — agreed to partner with him.

With his experience and charm, Nathu Kaka thrived. Old customers flocked to him. He expanded into wedding wear, and soon his modest store became a grand, two-storied landmark in Shivaji Park.

His revenge? **Success.**

92.

THE PROMOTION THAT NEVER CAME

Subbu had been eyeing a promotion for months. He worked late-nights, took on extra responsibilities, and did everything he could to prove himself. But when the announcement came, his colleague Sharma got the role instead.

Subbu was furious. "This is unfair! I worked harder than he did!" he fumed. His frustration consumed him — he couldn't focus, lost sleep, and snapped at colleagues and family. The stress was unbearable.

Guru, a family friend, invited Subbu for coffee. "You're stuck in resistance," Guru said. "You believe this *shouldn't* have happened — but it did. Fighting reality only drains you. What if you accepted it instead?"

"Accept it? So, I just give up?" Subbu retorted.

"Acceptance isn't surrender," Guru explained. "It means acknowledging what happened so you can move forward. Ask yourself — *what's next?* How can this situation serve you?"

Subbu reflected. Instead of dwelling on the unfairness, he met his boss for feedback. The boss was pleased that Subbu approached him. He explained that he expected his team to communicate concerns — otherwise, he wouldn't know about them.

Subbu improved his communication and built stronger connections. A few months later, another opportunity arose — this time, he was the obvious choice.

93.

DHIRUBHAI AMBANI'S STRESS REDUCTION STORY

Dhirubhai Ambani faced extreme stress due to violent political unrest in Aden. Instead of letting fear paralyze him, he applied the **SRI** (Sensible, Rational, Intelligent) approach to navigate his challenges.

1. **Sensible:** He realized that staying in Aden was unsafe and uncertain. Instead of overthinking or resisting change, he made a clear decision — leave everything behind and starts fresh in India.
2. **Rational:** Although his family wanted him to settle in Chorwad, he knew returning to his hometown wasn't the solution. His true goal was to build something meaningful, not seek temporary comfort.
3. **Intelligent:** He adapted to Mumbai's realities by living modestly and starting small. Rather than persisting with struggling businesses, he intelligently pivoted — using policy loopholes to create profitable trade strategies.

By following the SRI approach, he transformed stress into opportunity. When he couldn't raise funds from banks, he approached the public with innovative financial products. When the bear lobby hammered his stock in the market, he mobilized bulls to buy them, creating a scarcity that bankrupted many bears.

If we reflect on his career, we see that being sensible, rational, and intelligent helped him not only manage stress — but make history.

94.

STRESS HELPED SACHIN TENDULKAR

A 16-year-old schoolboy, Sachin Tendulkar, was selected to play against Pakistan in a Test series. During his debut in the Sialkot Test, India was struggling at 36 for 4. Facing the fiery pace trio—Imran Khan, Wasim Akram, and Waqar Younis — Sachin walked in to bat.

Waqar, eager to intimidate him, unleashed a brutal bouncer that smashed into Sachin's face. Blood poured from his broken nose. Navjot Sidhu, his co-batsman, and the Indian medical team urged him to retire hurt. Even Javed Miandad sneered, "Baccha (Boy), your nose is broken—how will you play? Go to the hospital."

But Sachin wiped away the blood, shook his head, and said, "I will play."

Shocked, the Pakistani bowlers targeted him with more bouncers. Pain seared through him. Time and again, he wiped blood from his face — but he stood his ground, defending fiercely and counterattacking with determination. With every ball, he proved he wasn't just a boy — he was a warrior.

By the end, he had saved the match for India. That day, Sachin didn't just survive — he announced himself to the world. Stress didn't break him. It made him. Had he walked away, history would have been different. But he stood tall—and became a legend.

95.

COPING WITH THE DELAY IN THE JUDICIAL PROCESS

Sunny was growing increasingly frustrated by the legal battle he had been fighting for the last five years. Every hearing brought hope — followed by disappointment. The delays felt endless, and the system unfair. He felt both helpless and angry at the same time. He was stressed.

One day, at a Stress Buster Meet-Up, Guru — who was a lawyer by education — sat beside him and explained:
"Justice is a process. You feel you are right, and the other person feels they are right. For justice to prevail, statements from both parties need to be taken. There are petitions, replies, rejoinders, evidence to be checked, and cross-examinations, if required. The country is huge, with millions of cases clogging the system. Some things take time not because they are denied — but because they must be fair."

"In the meantime, don't stop living. Focus on what you can control — your work, career, mental peace — and build what you can while the system works in its own way."

Sunny realized his stress wasn't just about the delay — but about his resistance to it. He started focusing on things he could control: his job, his skills, and his well-being. He accepted things as they were, not as he would have liked them to be.

One day, the verdict arrived — and justice was served. But more importantly, Sunny had moved forward in life instead of waiting in frustration.
Justice may be delayed, but your progress need not be.

96.

HOW ELON MUSK REDUCED STRESS

Elon Musk's early life was anything but easy. Born in South Africa, he witnessed his parents' difficult marriage and eventual divorce. His mother moved to Canada, leaving young Elon with his father, with whom he had a strained relationship. At school, he was an introverted, awkward child, often bullied by seniors.

To cope, Elon immersed himself in computer programming. At just 12, he sold his first video game for $500. The passion became his refuge from stress — keeping his mind engaged in building, learning, and innovating.

At age 17, he left for Canada, hoping to reunite with his mother, but no one was there to meet him. Alone in a new country, he checked into a youth hostel and took up survival jobs while studying at Queen's University. He later transferred to the University of Pennsylvania and then briefly attended Stanford before dropping out.

Rejected by Netscape, he started his own company, even sleeping in his office to make it succeed. That company led to X.com, which evolved into PayPal. He then reinvested his earnings into Tesla, SpaceX, and other ventures.

For Musk, stress relief wasn't about slowing down — it was about the relentless pursuit of his vision, keeping him too busy to dwell on hardships.

97.

MR. SHETTY'S TRANSFORMATION

Mr. Shetty was drowning in stress. Running his restaurant had become a nightmare — sky high tax and licence fees, a 10% VAT burden, and illegal competitors selling liquor at cheaper rates. He felt trapped, battling authorities who ignored his complaints while harassing him instead. Labor shortages only added to his troubles. His health suffered — high blood pressure, sugar levels, and acidity. Frustration made him short-tempered, and his family bore the brunt. His biggest heartbreak? His son refused to take over the business after witnessing his father's struggles.

One evening, his friend Guru — also a restaurateur — sat down with Mr. Shetty and his son. Instead of offering sympathy, Guru challenged the young man, "Use your intelligence. Think out of the box."

After much brainstorming, his son proposed a radical shift — turning their business into a Mangalorean seafood specialty restaurant: *FISHLY.*

Guru kept pushing: "Why would customers come to you?" "How would you be different from other restaurants?"

Those questions led to a clear strategy. They sourced the best fish from Sassoon Docks, used his grandmother's secret recipe, and marketed it on social media. Food bloggers raved. Business boomed. Mr. Shetty surrendered his liquor license, saved a fortune, and found peace. His health improved, his staff stayed, and most importantly — his son proudly took over.

98.

GOD IS TESTING ME

Diya was born into a wealthy, conservative family. She fell in love with a flashy young man and insisted on marrying him. Her family warned her, begged her, and finally disowned her. But she followed her heart.

Reality was cruel. Her husband had expected wealth. When he got nothing, he turned abusive. The insults, the beatings — she endured it all, whispering, "God is testing me."

Her daughter was born with a rare spinal condition where her neck was always tilted to one side, touching her shoulder. Doctor visits and physiotherapy were frequent, time-consuming, and expensive. But she endured, smiling and whispering, "God is testing me."

Her husband abandoned her and her daughter. From a palatial mansion, she moved to a dingy chawl. She struggled to survive, selling snacks to feed them and cover rising medical and schooling costs.

Then came cancer. A lump in her breast confirmed her worst fear. Treatments drained her, and she lost all her hair. But she kept going — through poverty, threats, and pain. Her faith was her anchor. "God is testing me."

Years later, her daughter earned a 100% scholarship and studied at a top American university. Today, her daughter is Managing Director of the India operations of a large multinational and owns a huge apartment at Malabar Hill. But Diya refuses to reside with her. She prefers to stay at the same dingy chawl—mentoring young students.

99.

PARESH MISHRA'S STRUGGLE

Paresh Mishra grew up in a small, close-knit town where dreams of stardom were rare. Yet, his passion for acting was undeniable. When he secured admission to the National School of Drama, it felt like a miracle. His family, though sceptical, borrowed heavily to support his dream.

But after graduation, reality hit hard. Rejection after rejection shattered his confidence. A year passed without a break. The pressure to send money home for loan repayment became unbearable. His family's belief began to fade. Stress consumed him.

In his darkest hour, he met a *Stress Support Guide* who gently said, "Simplify *your struggle by acceptance. Every newcomer in the industry has to go through it. The people who succeed are people who don't give up.* De-risk your dream. Build support. Exercise to flush out stress. Reflect daily. Journal your thoughts. Breathe deeply. Talk to God. Let faith carry what effort cannot."

Paresh took the advice to heart. He started driving for Uber. One day, a passenger complained over the phone, "No actor fits in the Bihari gangster role. Everyone talks like Shahrukh. As soon as the call ended, Paresh responded – in flawless Bihari accent. I am trained actor from NSD," he said. The passenger smiled, took his number and called him for an audition the next day. Paresh got the role. The web series became a massive hit - so did he. His struggle found its stage.

100.

HOW DONALD TRUMP REDUCED STRESS

In the high-pressure world of real estate and politics, Donald Trump often faced immense stress — billions at stake, lawsuits looming, media criticism pouring in. But during a rare interview, he shared a simple yet powerful approach to reducing stress: single-minded focus.

Trump said, "I don't let ten problems cloud my mind. I deal with one big thing at a time — like building a tower, one floor at a time." Six times, his companies went through bankruptcy. Instead of panicking, he blocked out the noise and focused on solutions. He reflected deeply, consulted key advisors, avoided negative media, and concentrated solely on restructuring deals. Even when there was strong resistance to his proposals, he stayed calm.

He also used physical symbols to stay grounded — like carrying a small piece of marble from Trump Tower in his pocket. It reminded him: *You've built before; you'll build again.* That small object brought him calm amidst chaos.

His takeaway? Stress multiplies when we try to solve everything at once. But if you focus like a laser and tackle the biggest problem first, the rest often falls into place. Keep faith in your past wins and stress transforms into energy. He turned crisis into comeback — with focus, faith, and confidence.